The New
Enchantment of America
TEXAS

By Allan Carpenter

CHILDRENS PRESS, CHICAGO

ACKNOWLEDGMENTS

For assistance in the preparation of the revised edition, the author thanks:
Consultant CAROL J. CAREFOOT, Reference Archivist, Texas State Library; ELMER C. WHID-DON Jr., Chief of Media Relations, Texas Tourist Development Agency; and RICHARD H. PIERCE, Manager, Travel Development, State Department of Highways and Public Transportation.

American Airlines— Anne Vitaliano, Director of Public Relations; *Capitol Historical Society,* Washington, D. C.; *Newberry Library,* Chicago, Dr. Lawrence Towner, Director; *Northwestern University Library,* Evanston, Illinois; *United Airlines*—John P. Grember, Manager of Special Promotions; Joseph P. Hopkins, Manager, News Bureau.

UNITED STATES GOVERNMENT AGENCIES: *Department of Agriculture*—Robert Hailstock, Jr., Photography Division, Office of Communication; Donald C. Schuhart, Information Division, Soil Conservation Service. *Army*—Doran Topolosky, Public Affairs Office, Chief of Engineers, Corps of Engineers. *Department of Interior*—Louis Churchville, Director of Communications; EROS Space Program—Phillis Wiepking, Community Affairs; Charles Withington, Geologist; Mrs. Ruth Herbert, Information Specialist; Bureau of Reclamation; National Park Service—Fred Bell and the individual sites; Fish and Wildlife Service—Bob Hines, Public Affairs Office. *Library of Congress*—Dr. Alan Fern, Director of the Department of Research; Sara Wallace, Director of Publications; Dr. Walter W. Ristow, Chief, Geography and Map Division; Herbert Sandborn, Exhibits Officer. *National Archives*—Dr. James B. Rhoads, Archivist of the United States; Albert Meisel, Assistant Archivist for Educational Programs; David Eggenberger, Publications Director; Bill Leary, Still Picture Reference; James Moore, Audio-Visual Archives. *United States Postal Service*—Herb Harris, Stamps Division.

For assistance in the preparation of the first edition, the author thanks:
Consultant Dr. M.G. Bowden, Principal, Casis School, Austin; Texas State Historical Association; Texas Highway Department; Tom H. Taylor, Director, Travel and Information Division; R.P. Jeffrey, Promotion Director, Dallas *Morning News;* Texas Industrial Commission; and The *Texas Outlook.*

Illustrations on the preceding pages:
Cover photograph: Palo Duro State Park, James P. Rowan

Page 1: Commemorative stamps of historic interest
Pages 2-3: Austin Municipal Auditorium, Austin Chamber of Commerce
Page 3: (Map) USDI Geological Survey
Pages 4-5: El Paso area, EROS Space Photo, USDI Geological Survey, EROS Data Center

Project Editor, Revised Edition:
 Joan Downing
Assistant Editor, Revised Edition:
 Mary Reidy

Library of Congress Cataloging in Publication Data

Carpenter, John Allan, 1917-
 Texas.

(His The new enchantment of America)
 1. Texas—Juvenile literature.
 I. Title. II. Series.
F386.3.C27   976.4   78-18430
ISBN 0-516-04143-6

Contents

The Surrender of Santa Anna *painted by William Henry Huddle.
Sam Houston was very generous in his treatment of Santa Anna,
considering the hundreds Santa Anna had massacred.*

A True Story to Set the Scene

THE WATERLOO OF THE WEST

It was a simple meeting between two men. One lay wounded under a great oak tree; the other stood, wearing a blue smock and red slippers. This meeting proved to be one of the most dramatic and extraordinary events in the history of the Americas—and certainly one of the most interesting stories of the enchantment of Texas.

Both men had taken part in a battle. One had been severely wounded in the leg, and lay in great pain. The other had fled in panic with the defeated forces. He had tried to escape through the deep woods along the banks of a bayou. When he saw a squad of the enemy approaching, commanded by James A. Sylvester, he had tried to hide in the brambles, then pleading for mercy, he was taken prisoner, and brought back to camp to join the other prisoners.

His captors, however, were in for a great surprise. When this apparently simple and unimpressive man was thrown in with the other prisoners, they drew back in awe, crying, "El Presidente! El Presidente!" Only then did his captors realize who he was.

He was brought before the man lying under the oak tree, General Sam Houston, Commander-in-Chief of the Army of the new Republic of Texas. General Houston had been wounded at the Battle of San Jacinto.

Drawing himself erect, the prisoner proclaimed proudly in Spanish, "I am General Antonio Lopez de Santa Anna, Commander-in-Chief of the Army of Operations, President of Mexico, and prisoner of war at your disposal."

A gasp went up from the Texans crowded around General Houston. Then muttering angrily, they tried to close in on the man who had been responsible for massacring hundreds of their comrades at the Alamo and Goliad. But Houston held them back. Indeed, this was a tremendous and useful triumph. The proud, haughty, arrogant, fierce, contemptuous, wicked, blood-thirsty Santa Anna, dictator of all Mexico, was a helpless captive. The one man who could end the war was in their power.

Santa Anna began to bargain for his freedom. "That man may consider himself born to no mean future who has vanquished the Napoleon of the West," the prisoner said. "Now it remains for him to be generous to the vanquished."

"What right have you to plead for mercy when you showed none at the Alamo?" Houston demanded.

"I had orders from my government to execute all prisoners taken bearing arms."

"You were the government," Houston thundered. "A dictator has no superior. Your butchery at the Alamo and Goliad has no equal for cruelty, and it cannot be justified under any pretext!"

Santa Anna looked fearfully at the soldiers, who were drawing closer. Then General Houston declared, "You must write an order at once demanding that all your troops in Texas leave the state forthwith, returning to Mexico."

"This I will do immediately," murmured the dictator.

The historic interview was over. From that time on, Texas was free.

Lay of the Land

WHAT IS TEXAS REALLY LIKE?

State officials took a nationwide survey in 1964 and discovered to their surprise that 87 percent of the nation thought Texas was a flat and arid desert. An incredible 90 percent believed that the whole of Texas was a flat and unvaried plain. Only 3 percent of non-Texans polled knew that there are mountains in Texas.

Actually, there is probably more variety to be found in Texas than in any other state. There are rich farm lands with plentiful rainfall, plantation lands like those of the deep South, bayou country, tropical islands, great stretches of ocean beach, evergreen and hardwood forests, and jungle-like thickets abounding in orchids.

Granite cliffs, deep, dark canyons, and lovely valleys all grace the Texas scene. And, of course, there are the plains, Texas' beloved ranges, stretching to far horizons, and there are arid deserts like gigantic sandboxes.

Also, there are mighty rivers and lakes. Most incredible of all to many people is the fact that Texas has more inland water than any other state except Alaska. The inland water area of Texas covers 4,499 square miles (about 11,650 square kilometers).

One of the principal reasons for this great diversity is Texas' unique geographical location. It is within all of the four major divisions of the North American continent. Only in Texas do all of these four divisions come together. The Great Plains, which sweep across much of the heart of the continent, ranging north across the United States and far on into Canada, end in Texas. The Trans-Pecos region of Texas is a part of the great mountain system, which marches almost unbroken from Alaska to the southern tip of South America. The Central Plain, typical of neighboring Oklahoma and extending on through Kansas, Nebraska, the Dakotas, and into the Canadian provinces, are part of mid-Texas. Great areas of the Coastal Plain make up the fourth major division of Texas.

Even within these divisions there is an enormous variety of natural features due to the vast size of each section.

El Capitan, the second highest mountain in Texas.

NATURAL FEATURES

The Texas of today is formed somewhat like a series of gigantic steps. The various plains regions are separated by interesting cliffs called escarpments.

The natural boundary between the Coastal Plains region and the Central Plains is called the Balcones Escarpment because the early Spaniards thought it looked like a balcony. Cap Rock Escarpment is the name given to the natural boundary separating the Central Plains and High Plains.

Mountains really do exist in Texas. The highest are the Guadalupe Mountains, and Guadalupe Peak at 8,751 feet (about 2,670 meters) is the highest in the state. El Capitan is Texas' second highest.

The mountains around Van Horn are noted for their exceptional beauty. Fort Davis, surrounded by the Davis Mountains, is the highest town in Texas. One of the country's great granite shields is found in the Granite Mountain area.

Many unusual features are located throughout the state. The coastline is almost entirely protected by a series of very narrow islands and thin peninsulas, like the loose peel of a Texas grapefruit. This formation of coast is similar to that of many of the Atlantic Coast states. Padre Island is the most famous of these slivers of sand.

12

Another area of sand in Sandhills State Park, near Monahans, is possibly more like the Sahara Desert than any other part of the United States.

A 10-acre (about 4 hectares) crater near Odessa marks the spot where a meteor of nickel and iron, weighing an estimated 625 tons (about 567 metric tons), crashed far into the earth in a cloud of smoke and shower of sparks.

Other holes in the ground are the Hueco Tanks, not far from El Paso. These are eroded deep into the solid granite and many a parched traveler has been delighted to find that the Hueco Tanks hold large supplies of rain water for extended periods.

WATER FOR A THIRSTY LAND

Historic and romantic rivers form much of the boundary of Texas. To the south and west flows a river which is grand by its very name, the Rio Grande. Someone has said that the Rio Grande is a mile (about 1.6 kilometers) wide and a foot (about 30 centimeters) deep—too thin to plow and too thick to drink. It is the fourth or fifth

The beach at Padre Island.

Lake Arrowhead

longest river on the continent. To the north the fabled Red River forms 440 miles (about 708 kilometers) of the boundary between Texas and Oklahoma. Much of the eastern boundary of Texas is shaped by the Sabine River.

The major river between the Red and the Rio Grande is the Brazos. Its full name is *Brazos de Dios,* which means "the arms of God." Other Texas rivers on the list of principal rivers of the U. S. Geological Survey are the Neches, Nueces, Trinity, Colorado, and Canadian.

The clear-flowing San Antonio River is so winding that the Indians called it by a name which means "drunken-old-man-going-home-at-night." While it does not have a large volume, the springs which bring it into being, not far from the city of San Antonio, keep its flow remarkably even. Another spring-fed river is the San Marcos. Its springs jet out in a remarkable manner from fissures in the rocks.

The shortest river in Texas, the Comal, begins and ends within the limits of a single city. The Comal begins in a spring in one part of New Braunfels and ends at the Guadalupe River, still within the city limits. It flows full and clear for all its 2½ miles (about 4 kilometers).

One of the world's largest artesian springs is Comanche, near Fort Stockton. Del Rio is famous for its springs, which make it a green oasis in the desert. The exact source of the water flowing daily from San Felipe springs, near Del Rio, has never been satisfactorily explained. Mud geysers and sulphur springs are found at Palmetto State Park.

When the program of creating artificial lakes is completed, there will be 126 reservoirs in Texas, making the total of 213 natural lakes and reservoirs. The largest body of water wholly within Texas is

14

Lake Sam Rayburn. Caddo Lake, Texoma, Corpus Christi, Whitney, Toledo Bend, Livingston, and the Highland Lakes are others either wholly or partly in Texas.

IN AN ANCIENT AGE

During the unknown millions of years in which Texas was formed, the land went through at least six submergings and uprisings. Each time, new features saw the light of day. In some places wind and water have cut through the rocks, exposing the different layers. Geologists can read the story of the earth as if it had been written. This is true in Palo Duro Canyon where the forces of nature have been carving for ninety million years. At least four different geologic ages have been exposed in these eroded formations.

About two hundred and fifty million years ago, a mighty prehistoric mountain range stretched across the middle of Texas from southwest to northeast. This, of course, has long since disappeared.

Rockwall is a strange formation of rock near the town of that name. It goes deep into the earth in an arrangement as thin and vertical as a wall. Embedded in the sides of this wall are many fossils. The origin of this strange formation is unknown.

In the many twistings and turnings, risings and fallings of the earth over the ages, the bodies of sea creatures, shellfish, animals, and plants were pressed together by the weight of the earth or water above. Today these remains are among the most useful resources available to man, forming such products as coal, sandstone, and, most important, petroleum and natural gas.

THE LONGEST BORDER

One of the most interesting geographical features of Texas is man-made and not natural. The border between Texas and Oklahoma is the longest boundary between any two states of the United States.

Pictographs found in the Devil's River area.

Footsteps on the Land

A CAVE ON THE RANGE

A sleepy town west of the Big Bend country can truthfully claim to be one of the most distinguished settlements in America. This is the adobe village of Presidio. There has been a town or village in this area for more than 10,000 years. Some authorities claim that Presidio may be the oldest town on the continent.

Human beings have lived in Texas for at least 25,000 years, probably much longer. The most ancient of these peoples are known as Paleo-Americans, and they left behind some distinctive stone spear points. With these spears they hunted fierce, long-tusked mammoths, prehistoric camels, and tiny, prehistoric horses.

Prehistoric peoples of east Texas, who lived about 12,000 years ago, raised many varied earthen mounds. Some of these may still be seen today.

In the Panhandle, prehistoric men lived in underground houses of somewhat advanced construction with walls of limestone slabs set in adobe. Shumla Cave Shelters served as home for the West Texas cave dwellers, who lived from 2,000 to 8,000 years ago. It is generally thought that these ancient people had a rather high degree of culture. They wove baskets and cloth, and braided rope and twine. They used the atlatl, a kind of throwing weapon. Another weapon was the rabbit stick, which was similar to the Australian boomerang. Some infant burials of these people have been found with the tiny bodies laid to rest in well-made cradles.

Possibly more recently, a prehistoric people lived in the Panhandle. Their customs somewhat resembled those of the Pueblo culture. Pueblo type ruins have been found on the banks of the Canadian River near Amarillo.

Among the most interesting and revealing traces left by ancient peoples are the mounds called kitchen middens. These could be described as trash heaps, where the refuse of everyday living was dumped. When Europeans came, they found the Indians depositing trash on very high mounds. After some of these were excavated, it was found that the same mounds had been used for thousands of years.

In their deepest parts, the kitchen middens of Central Texas can be traced back to what is called the Archaic Culture of around 4,000 B.C. When archeologists dig into these, they find bones, shells, and other refuse. Experts can do much to reconstruct the life of these people from the things they left behind. This is the only means we have of finding out about ancient people, because they left no written records.

Other interesting remains in Texas include the Medicine Mounds near Lake Pauline, Burned Rock kitchen middens, and the mounds of Nacogdoches. Fine discoveries of prehistoric tools have been made in the region between Roscoe and Muleshoe.

The people who lived in Texas just before the Europeans came were a part of what is called Neo-American Culture. They farmed, created pottery, and made and used bows and arrows with fine, light stone points.

Another record left by ancient people is the picture writing or pictographs which they painted on cave walls and the smooth rocks of bluffs, buttes, and other rock formations. For the most part, these are not yet readable by our scholars. Some of these were 17 feet (about 5 meters) long. Paint Rock near Ballinger is known for its pictographs. Some of these are ancient and some fairly modern, showing the devil as described to the Indians by the early missionaries.

Picture stories which were carved into the rock itself are called petroglyphs. Deep rock carvings of this type cover a large area of limestone surface near Shumla.

LAND OF TEJAS, THE FRIENDLY LAND

During a great drought in Texas, a little Indian girl became concerned that her people might starve. She tried to think what she might do to make the gods look on them with favor. Some great sacrifice was necessary. Suddenly she knew what it must be. She would burn her favorite doll as a sacrifice. A gentle rain came during the night, and in the morning the ground where the doll's ashes fell was covered with a beautiful blue flower. This, according to the Indian legend, is the origin of Texas' state flower—the bluebonnet.

Much of the history and lore of Texas has to do with the Indians. In fact, the Indians gave Texas its name. Some early explorers asked a group of Indians the name of their group. The Indians replied that they were "Tejas." The explorers did not know that this was the Indian word meaning "friendly people," and not their name. Over the years, the word came into general use to describe the area and its people, and has become the "Texas" that we know today.

When Europeans first came to that land, there were at least 30,000 Indians in the present area of Texas. Some experts say there may have been closer to 130,000.

On the coast, the Gulf groups included the Attacapas, Deadoses, Arkokiasa, Bidais, and Karankawa. The Karankawa were cannibals, and gnawed human bones were found in their refuse piles. The Karankawa had a strange habit of spending most of the daytime hours in the leafy treetops, coming down to the ground for night raids on terrified neighbors.

When the Spaniards first came to the area, the largest group of Indians living there was the Caddo. There were three main groupings of the Caddo: the group which actually called itself Caddo, the Hasinai Confederacy, and the Wichita. These confederacies covered much of north-central, central, and eastern Texas.

A field of bluebonnets, the state flower of Texas.

The Caddo group included the Grand Caddo, Little Caddo, Adaes, Nachitoches, and Natsoo. The Hasinai groups were made up of Nadoco, Neche, Heinai, Nasoni, and Nacogdoches. Most of these raised crops, lived in permanent adobes, and had a fairly high standard of culture. Not so advanced were the Wichita Caddo, living near the Red River, including Tawakinis (Tehuacana), Taovayo, and Yscani. The Caddo groups are generally thought to be the southwesternmost of America's mound-building Indians.

One of the earliest explorers gives an interesting description of the "Tejas" clan: ". . . very intelligent; the women are well made and modest. . . . They wear shoes and buskins made of tanned skin. The women wear cloaks over their small under-petticoats, with sleeves gathered up at the shoulders, all of skin."

In central Texas lived the Xaraname, Tamique, and Tonkawa, and south into Mexico were the Coahuiltecan. West of the Pecos lived the fierce Lipan Apache, and the most consistently warlike of all Texas Indians—the Mescalero Apache.

One of the earliest explorers described the Apache: "They go about with the buffalo, and eat the meat raw and drink the blood of the cows they kill. They tan the skins with which all of the people clothe themselves." The Apache were implacable foes of Europeans, and from 1681 until 1890 they carried on what has been described as history's longest war—the Apache War.

Another group bitterly opposing the Europeans was the Comanche, a branch of Shoshone. In early times they lived in the upper Panhandle, but they advanced rapidly across much of the state.

These, then, were the native people of Texas found by the Europeans who were later to become their conquerors.

COMING OF THE COLORFUL ONES

A dashing young man in Spanish armor, with a bright feather in his helmet, urged his splashing horse out of the Rio Grande up onto the banks where El Paso now stands. Following him across the river was one of the most extraordinary processions in history.

His wife and sixteen high-born Spanish señoritas came in their sturdy ox carts. A hundred and fifty gentlemen-at-arms in full battle dress, riding beautiful horses, carrying swords, shields, and lances; two hundred infantrymen with crossbows and arquebuses (guns); three hundred Spanish settlers; three hundred Mexican Indians, all converts to Christianity; eight hundred sheep, six hundred longhorn cattle, and four hundred extra horses—all crossed the Rio Grande.

When everyone had reached the northern back, the young man, Don Juan de Oñate, formally claimed possession for the king of Spain everything to the north, east, and west. This was the first time present-day Texas had ever been claimed formally. The year was 1598.

The six priests who came with the procession, carrying all the supplies and equipment necessary for their offices, said mass. A longhorn was slaughtered and offered as a gift to the wondering Indians of the region, who ate it raw.

That night, in celebration, Senora Oñate and her lovely ladies-in-waiting and some of the gentlemen of the court staged a play in the wilderness. This was probably the first play ever presented in the United States.

It is interesting to note the wardrobe Don Juan de Oñate carried with him—seven velvet coats (three yellow and four purple), five suits of armor (two of plate and three of chain), eleven pairs of satin pants, and sixteen pairs of genuine silk stockings. It is no wonder that the Indians of the region told the wonders of this procession for generations to come.

Oñate was not the first European to set foot on Texas soil. In fact, during the years from 1519 to 1731 ninety-two separate expeditions crossed into Texas.

Alonzo Alvarez de Piñeda mapped most of the coast of the Gulf of Mexico in 1519, and made such discoveries as Corpus Christi Bay and the mouth of the Rio Grande. A few years later, he established a colony at the mouth of a river he called Rio de las Palmas (River of the Palms), which is thought to have been the Rio Grande. This colony was soon abandoned.

A great Spanish expedition from Mexico under Panfilo de Narváez was shipwrecked in Florida. The survivors under Alvar Núñez Cabeza de Vaca built crude boats and tried to sail back to Mexico in 1528. Their frail crafts were wrecked on the Texas coast, probably near Galveston. The survivors were held captive by the cannibal Karankawa. De Vaca was saved from being eaten by impressing the Indians with his power as a medicine man.

After seven years de Vaca and three other Spaniards escaped on foot, and began one of the most incredible adventures in history. They wandered across Texas, passing present-day El Paso in about 1536, and eventually reached their countrymen in Lower California.

De Vaca told wonderful stories about the land he had visited and the stories he heard of the Seven Cities of Cibola, wealthy lands of cultured people, gold and jewels, and the equally fabulous Gran Quivira.

A noble Spaniard, Francisco Vasquez de Coronado, led a great expedition across the Rio Grande in 1541 to try and find these wealthy people, and strip them of their possessions. This was a wild goose chase for, of course, nothing like these wealthy cities existed.

As the Coronado party crossed the high plains of Texas, their historian wrote, "Who would believe that a thousand horses and five hundred of our cows, and more than five thousand rams and ewes, and more than fifteen hundred friendly Indians and servants, in traveling over these plains, would leave no more trace where they had passed than if nothing had been there?"

After failing to find any wealth to take back to the high Spanish rulers of Mexico, Coronado returned in disgrace. But he left a legacy in Texas which has lasted until this day. Some of the horses and cows of the expedition escaped or were captured by Indians. Under the ideal conditions there, the animals multiplied, and later provided whole new industries in wild cattle and horses.

BEGINNINGS OF SETTLEMENT

The first permanent settlement of Europeans in present-day Texas, called Ysleta, was established in 1682, not far from El Paso.

22

Texas' first and most famous mission, San Antonio de Valero (the Alamo), echoes the historic past in modern surroundings.

At one time this was on the Mexican side of the Rio Grande, but the river shifted its course placing it on the northern side.

In 1685, the famed French explorer, René Robert Cavelier, Sieur de La Salle, founder of Illinois, sailed with a force of ships and men to set up a French colony in Louisiana, but he got off course and sailed into Lavaca Bay. One of his ships was wrecked, but the party went on up the bay and landed at a river he called Les Vaches, or The Cows, because of the buffalo he saw along the banks. Two of his men were killed there by the Karankawa Indians.

On the bay, La Salle built a fort called St. Louis. In 1687 one of his own men murdered La Salle on an exploring expedition.

The Spanish suspected that La Salle went off his course intentionally, and that he planned all the time to establish a colony on land claimed by the Spanish. Alarmed at this, they hurriedly made plans to move into various parts of the lands they claimed west of the Mississippi River.

In 1690 Spanish Captain Alonso de Leon pushed up toward Fort St. Louis, only to find that the French had abandoned it. He established Mission San Francisco de Los Tejas near present-day Weches, but this was soon abandoned also.

A year later Don Domingo Terande de Los Rios and Father Damian Massanet found an Indian village on the banks of a river. They raised a cross there and established a mission settlement which grew into the historic city of San Antonio.

In the next forty years about a dozen missions were established in

Texas. They became outposts of Spanish civilization, each protected by fortresses called presidios. The manual work of the missions was carried on mostly by Indians from Mexico who were brought in for the purpose. Altogether, during Spanish rule in Texas thirty-two missions were established.

Still, after about a hundred years of work in the missions, there were only about 7,000 Europeans living in the vast area of present-day Texas. By this time, Spain's power was slipping fast both at home and in the Americas.

SOME WOULD-BE CONQUERORS

In 1801 an American named Philip Nolan went into Texas with about twenty men. He said his only purpose was to hunt wild horses, but the Spanish authorities became suspicious and had Nolan and most of his men killed. Nolan's ears were then cut off and sent to the Spanish governor as proof of his death.

When the United States purchased Louisiana from France in 1803, Spain became still more disturbed about her hold on Texas. Americans claimed their newly bought territory stretched clear to the Rio Grande, and this was disputed until 1819 when the Sabine and Red rivers were set as the northern and eastern boundaries of Texas.

Before this happened, however, the United States and Spain had agreed to set up a neutral strip on either side of the Sabine, where neither side would govern. Wanted men and desperadoes of almost every type found a haven in this neutral ground where there was no government.

A former U.S. Army officer, Augustus Magee, marched out of the neutral strip with an army of outlaws with vague notions of capturing Texas, or even all Mexico! They called themselves the Republican Army of the North, and their symbol was the Green Flag. They captured Nacogdoches in July, 1812, then Goliad, and finally the capital, San Antonio. But Magee was already dead, although the manner of his death is not certain, and the invaders were later captured and most of them killed. Even though this invasion had no lasting effect, a good many authorities feel that the Green Flag should be added to the list of flags which have flown over Texas. Some feel that the course of Texas history might have been much different if Magee had lived.

Much more powerful, however, was another rebel in Texas territory, the notorious pirate Jean Lafitte. He and his men sailed in and took possession of Galveston in 1817. There he built a fortress-home called Maison Rouge (the Red House). Lafitte called his settlement Campeachy, and it became a pirate kingdom, with Lafitte known as the lord of Galveston. During his reign, Lord Lafitte captured and looted more than a hundred Spanish ships. He permitted a merciless business in slaves, and lived up to the reputation of a bloodthirsty pirate.

A hurricane and battle with the Karankawa Indians reduced his power, however, and soon a U. S. cutter came to port and demanded that Lafitte leave. He set fire to Campeachy and sailed off.

Another unsuccessful attempt by an American to capture Texas was tried by Dr. James Long. After some success with a force of soldiers from the neutral ground, he was captured and taken to Mexico City. There he was just in time to see Spain give up in Mexico, and the Mexican Republic established. Dr. Long was showered with honors for helping to conquer the Spaniards in Texas, but he was assassinated before he could return to Texas.

AMERICAN SETTLEMENT

The next American who went to Texas was entirely different. Moses Austin did not have conquest in mind. Instead, he made the long, tiring trip to San Antonio to get permission to bring a group of American settlers into Texas.

Moses Austin's son, Stephen, wrote an interesting memorandum about this trip: "My father, after a fatiguing journey on horseback of more than 800 miles (about 1,287 kilometers), reached Bexar (San Antonio) in November. His reception by the Governor was discouraging. . . . The Governor not only refused to read the papers my father presented as evidence of his having formerly been a Spanish subject in Louisiana, but . . . ordered that he leave Texas immediately.

"In crossing the public square he accidentally met the Baron de Bastrop. They had seen each other once before in the United States. . . . His influence with the Government was considerable. . . . In the Baron's dwelling the object of my father's visit to the Capital of Texas was explained. . . . The benefits that would accrue from the contemplated colony were apparent to Baron de Bastrop at the very first view.

"As my father was really unwell . . . a suspension of the order for his immediate departure was obtained. And at the end of a week, the Governor recommended a petition from my father . . . asking for permission to introduce and settle three hundred families from the United States of America at any point in Texas which my father might select.

"Thus a mere accident had prevented the total failure of the first preliminary step. . . . The hardships and privations of my father's return were so severe that he was taken with fever and confined to his bed for three weeks." He never recovered and died in 1821, about six months after he left Texas.

Stephen F. Austin, 1798-1836, "Father of Texas"—from a portrait by Robert Joy, San Jacinto Memorial Monument and Museum.

Before Moses Austin died, Stephen Austin promised his father that he would carry on his plans for American settlement in Texas. True to his word, Stephen Austin arranged to bring three hundred families to settle on the Colorado and Brazos rivers. They called their settlements Washington-on-the-Brazos and Columbus-on-the-Colorado. Meanwhile, Mexico (including Texas) became independent of Spain in 1821, and Austin had to make the tremendously long trip to Mexico City to get the new government to confirm his grant. This was the beginning of Anglo-American Texas.

Austin was a remarkable administrator. He chose his settlers carefully for their good character, ability, and determination. They moved ahead with great vigor to build homes, prepare farms, and arrange for protection from the Indians. San Felipe de Austin (in present-day Austin County) was laid out as capital of the Austin colony, and carefully chosen settlers continued to come.

The Austin colony was independent of the local Mexican government, and could govern itself. In many ways the Mexican government was extremely liberal to the new American settlers. Mexico cancelled all the settlers' past debts, and forgave them all taxes for a five-year period.

However, the settlers were required to become citizens of Mexico, and all settlers in the colonies were compelled to become Catholic. Neither of these requirements seemed to bother the settlers, who were apparently quite flexible as to their citizenship and religion.

There were few priests in Texas, and it might be months before one would visit. All awaited the event with anticipation, because those who had not been baptized or married in the Catholic faith would have these rites performed. These mass ceremonies were regarded as the most exciting events in the lives of the colonists.

One wedding in 1828 was pictured by Noah Smithwick: "When young folks danced in those days, they danced. . . . They 'shuffled' and 'double-shuffled,' 'wired' and 'cut the pigeon's wing,' making the splinters fly. . . . The fiddle being rather too weak to make itself heard above the din of clattering feet, we had in another fellow a clevis and pin to strengthen the orchestra, and we had a most enjoyable time."

The Reverend Joseph L. Bays, a Baptist, was arrested for Protestant preaching, but over the years some other Protestant ministers did manage to preach occasionally. There was so little religion present that some predicted the Texas colonies would lapse into barbarism.

In the years after Stephen Austin's settlement, many other Americans were given the privilege of making settlements, as empresarios. The empresarios had full powers to set up militia, provide for laws and courts, and establish commerical centers.

Suddenly, in 1830, the Mexicans became alarmed by the situation they had created. Texas was remote from Mexico City. It was close to United States ports, and commerce was easy with the States. So Mexico passed a law limiting further American settlement, and discouraging trade with the United States.

From this time on, relations between Texans and the Mexican government grew worse. Settlers had no territorial government in Texas, and many rights were denied them, such as bail and jury trials. Clashes began to occur between Texan and Mexican forces.

In 1833 Texans held a convention at San Felipe proposing that Texas be created as a state under the Mexican system. They sent Stephen Austin to Mexico City to make this proposal, and asked a newcomer to Texas, Sam Houston, to head a convention to write a constitution for the proposed state.

At this time most Texans, including Austin, were not considering any move for independence from Mexico. This was not true of Sam Houston, however; when he left the United States to go to Texas, a

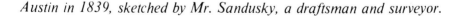

Austin in 1839, sketched by Mr. Sandusky, a draftsman and surveyor.

friend gave him a razor. "I accept the gift," Houston smiled, "and mark my words, if I have luck, this razor will some day shave the chin of the president of a republic."

Austin's experiences in Mexico City were memorable ones. Mexico was in turmoil. Santa Anna was president and was at work on plans to become a dictator. Austin could not get him to agree to make Texas either a state or a territory, so he started back. However, he had written a letter advising his friends in Texas to go ahead with their plan for a territory without waiting for permission from Mexico. This letter fell into Mexican hands, and Austin was thrown into a filthy jail where he was a prisoner for over a year.

Austin was released and returned to Texas in September of 1835. As soon as he arrived, he informed the Texans that in his opinion war was the only remedy for their problems. The first shots of that war came when the Mexican army was turned back at Gonzales as they tried to take back a cannon which the Texans had borrowed some time before.

The Texans elected Stephen Austin commander in chief. They set off to capture San Antonio, but it was too well defended, and they began a siege.

In November a convention met at San Felipe. They did not declare independence, but simply set up a new state of Mexico. Austin and two others were to go to the United States, asking for a loan and any other help they could get. With Austin away, Sam Houston was chosen as commander in chief. Someone said jokingly that this was because he had the only complete uniform in Texas. Actually, Houston possessed an excellent war record as an officer under General Andrew Jackson, who was then President of the United States.

Meanwhile the siege of San Antonio dragged on. Colonel Ben Milam called for volunteers to storm the town, and although only three hundred responded, they began the attack. Under heavy artillery fire from more than a thousand defenders, the attackers literally dug and cut their way through the adobe walls until they reached the Alamo, and overcame the artillery. This amazingly small force had captured the city, and Mexican General Perfecto de Cos surrendered. It was December, 1835. The Texans had lost only two men; unfortunately for the future course of the war, one of these was capable, courageous Ben Milam. As soon as Santa Anna heard of San Antonio's fall, he set off for Texas with a force of four to five thousand men.

Meanwhile, Dr. James Grant began to lead a foolhardy campaign into Mexico. He took with him most of the horses, provisions, ammunition wagons, and other supplies that would be needed to defend San Antonio against Santa Anna. Because Sam Houston advised caution, they deposed him from his command.

Before this, however, Houston had sent Jim Bowie with an order for the forces at San Antonio under Lieutenant Colonel William Barret Travis to withdraw to a safer position. But they could not do this because their wagons were gone.

On February 23, 1836, Santa Anna arrived at San Antonio with a force of thousands. Travis, whose forces had dwindled to 157 soldiers, plus some women and children, took refuge in an old mission called the Alamo. This mission had been abandoned in 1793, and although much of its roof had caved in its thick walls offered the greatest protection of any position in the city.

When Travis called for reinforcements, a force of thirty-two men from Gonzales under Captain Albert Martin managed to get through Santa Anna's lines to join the besieged Americans. This force has been named the thirty-two immortals.

For thirteen days the small force of less than two hundred withstood the Mexican attack. Colonel Travis wrote a letter from the Alamo, calling for support. He said, in part, "The enemy has demanded a surrender at discretion, otherwise, the garrison are to be put to the sword if the fort is taken—I have answered the demand with a cannon shot, and our flag still waves proudly from the walls—I shall never surrender or retreat. I call on you in the name of liberty and patriotism to come to our aid. . . . If this call is neglected, I am determined to sustain myself as long as possible and die like a soldier who never forgets what is due to his own honor and that of his country—victory or death. William Barret Travis."

On March 6, 1836, four to five thousand Mexicans charged the

Dawn at the Alamo, *painted by H.A. McArdle.*

Alamo. In spite of the odds, the brave defenders fought on. Jim Bowie, who was ill with pneumonia, fought from his cot. When the last shot was fired, every defender of the Alamo lay dead—including Jim Bowie, Davy Crockett, and Colonel Travis. One hundred and eighty-seven Texans were known to have died. But Santa Anna's victory was costly; before their deaths the defenders had killed sixteen hundred Mexicans.

The defense of the Alamo has been called one of the most heroic struggles in the annals of mankind.

As the siege of the Alamo was going on, another historic event was taking place at Washington-on-the-Brazos. A convention of Texans there prepared a declaration of independence making Texas an independent republic. Just four days before the Alamo fell, a constitution was adopted for the new republic. As provisional president they elected David G. Burnet, and restored Sam Houston as commander in chief.

Houston and his small army set out for San Antonio, but learning of the fall of the Alamo they began to retreat. Houston ordered Colonel James W. Fannin to retreat from Goliad with his 330 men, but Fannin refused. When the mighty forces of Santa Anna overcame him, Fannin surrendered on supposedly honorable terms. However, on Palm Sunday, the treacherous general ordered them all massacred. More than three hundred were killed in cold blood. Through the brave help of Señora Alvarez, wife of one of Santa Anna's officers, twenty-seven of the prisoners were able to escape death. There is little wonder that Señora Alvarez has become known as the angel of Goliad.

With about 30,000 Americans living in Texas at this time, Sam

31

Houston could not understand why so few volunteered to fight. But after the massacre of the Alamo and Travis' letter became known, the number of volunteers increased, and soon Houston was drilling about 1,600 men. However, when Santa Anna advanced, many settlers fled their homes in panic, and large numbers of volunteers left the army to help their families.

For forty days, Houston and his small army retreated, out-maneuvering General Santa Anna. Houston wrote, "My policy was to concentrate, retreat, and conquer." The provisional government of Texas fled to Galveston where a temporary capital was set up. When Houston reached Buffalo Bayou, he tore down Isaac Batterson's house for lumber to make a raft to get his ammunition across to San Jacinto.

Then Houston wrote, "This morning we are in preparation to meet Santa Anna. It is the only chance of saving Texas. From time to time I have looked for reinforcements in vain. . . . Texas could have started at least four thousand men. We will only have about seven hundred to march with. . . . We go to conquer. . . ."

Santa Anna had been expecting Houston to attack. When the attack did not come, he and his men lay down for their afternoon siesta. Then Houston called for the attack, with the cry, "Victory is certain. Trust in God and fear not. And remember the Alamo! Remember the Alamo!"

Overcome by surprise, the Mexicans were soundly defeated. Six hundred thirty were killed, 280 wounded and 730 captured. Only nine Texans were killed and thirty wounded, including General Houston who had been severely hurt in the leg.

The battle of San Jacinto, with its capture of President Santa Anna, has been called one of the decisive battles of world history.

A VERY INDEPENDENT REPUBLIC

In 1836, in their first national election as an independent republic, the people of Texas chose Sam Houston as president, with Mirabeau B. Lamar as vice-president. Stephen Austin was named secretary of

The Battle of San Jacinto, *by H.A. McArdle.*

state, but he died on December 27. They adopted the constitution prepared by the convention at Washington-on-the-Brazos. The people at this time also voted to request annexation of Texas as a state of the United States.

Many problems faced the infant country. It was poor, in debt, and Mexico was a continuing threat.

One of the problems was Santa Anna, who was held for six months before being returned to his country, after the so-called treaty of Velasco was signed. Actually, no peace treaty was ever signed with Mexico.

As time went by, various countries began to recognize the independence of the new country, including the United States, France, Belgium, Holland, Great Britain, and some of the German states.

Mirabeau B. Lamar was chosen to be the second president of the Republic of Texas in September, 1838. He is known as the Father of Education in Texas. He promoted the law to give each county three leagues of land for school purposes, and to set aside very large tracts for two future state universities.

Lamar was a strong supporter of the Texas navy. During the war for independence, Texas had possessed four ships, based at Galveston. They had done fine work in keeping Mexico from blockading the coast. After the republic was established, Mexico again threatened to blockade the coast, and the Texas navy sailed into Mexican waters, temporarily capturing a number of Mexican ports.

A commission to select a capital chose Austin in 1839. Workers putting up the new town had to be protected from Indians by armed guards. The unimposing first capitol building required a stockade for its protection.

President Lamar did not understand the Indians. He hated them so much that he disregarded treaties Sam Houston had made with his friends the Cherokee, and they were driven out during the Cherokee War.

The Comanches also were mistreated, and in 1840 they went on the warpath in the worst Indian raid in Texas history, sweeping in a path of death and destruction clear to the coast. The immediate danger was over when the Indians were defeated in the Battle of Plum Creek. However, some Indians continued to fight for many years.

During this period there was also constant danger of raids and attacks by Mexico. In 1842 two different Mexican expeditions attacked Texas, capturing San Antonio and other towns, but they finally withdrew. In answer to this, a Texas force of about three hundred commanded by Colonel W.S. Fisher crossed into Mexico and attacked the strong town of Mier. They fought well, but were defeated and captured.

On the way to Mexico City the Texas prisoners escaped at Salado. When they were caught, the Mexicans announced that as punishment for trying to escape, every tenth man would be executed. A most gruesome lottery was arranged for selecting those who would be killed. They put beans in a jar equal to the number of prisoners; every tenth bean was black. It is not difficult to imagine the scene. Men placed their hands in the jar, one by one. Those who drew the black beans of death were led away to be executed.

The remaining prisoners were taken to Mexico City and imprisoned. Only about thirty-five were eventually released.

Texas had another war in 1842. This was the comic Archives War. Sam Houston was again president, and he had the capital moved from Austin to Houston because of the Mexican threat. When he sent a messenger to bring the republic's supply of stationery from Austin to Houston, the people of Austin sheared the mane and tail of the horse, and sent the messenger back empty-handed. When another group tried to remove the government records secretly, the plan was discovered, and a group of Austin citizens captured the wagon carrying the documents and brought them back.

In 1844, under the new president, Anson Jones, the capital was returned to Austin.

A LONE STAR JOINS MANY

Texans had waited for ten years, as an independent nation, while the Congress and people of the United States argued about their request for statehood. Many in the United States bitterly opposed admitting a new slave state.

However, Congress adopted an offer for a treaty to be made with Texas with the following terms: the state would retain all its public lands; it would not become a territory as was the case with all other states outside the original thirteen; it would pay its own public debts. If Texas wished, it might choose to divide into a total of not more than five states. (Texas still has this right, but there is little chance that this will ever be done.)

A convention at Washington-on-the-Brazos drew up a proposed state constitution which was approved by the people of Texas. On December 29, 1845, Congress approved the constitution, and on

Pioneer Texas life is recreated in the fascinating Ranching Heritage Center, dedicated July 4, 1976, by Mrs. Lyndon B. Johnson, as a part of the Bicentennial celebration. The Picket and Sotol House, below, is typical of those made by resourceful pioneer ranchers.

that date Texas officially became the twenty-eighth state of the United States.

President Jones technically continued in office as the last president of the republic until February 19, 1846. On that date J. Pinckney Henderson was inaugurated as governor, with Sam Houston and Thomas J. Rusk as United States senators. Texas became the first and only state to be admitted to the Union by such arrangements.

The Lone Star flag of the Republic of Texas was lowered for the last time. This is the only state flag that at one time was the flag of a sovereign republic. The Stars and Stripes of the United States went up, and President Anson Jones proclaimed, "The Republic of Texas is no more!" "Long live the state of Texas" was the answer in the hearts of the people.

Presented to –
The Governor's mansion of Texas
during the administration of
Governor James V. Allred
by Temple Houston Morrow

Dallas, Texas
March 2, 1935

A portrait of Sam Houston by Freeman Thorpe.

Yesterday and Today

EARLY STATEHOOD

Mexico considered the annexation of Texas as an act of war. The first battle of the Mexican war was fought in Texas at Palo Alto on May 8, 1846. The end of the war marked the close of a long and tremendously important series of events which began with the triumph at San Jacinto. The territory of the United States was vastly increased with the addition of Texas, California, New Mexico, Arizona, Nevada, and parts of Colorado, Oklahoma, Kansas, Utah, and Wyoming.

In the period that followed, many foreign groups and religious groups found new homes in Texas. Large numbers of Germans came to establish Fredericksburg and New Braunfels. In 1855 more than two hundred French people arrived to set up their colony called La Reunion. Although this colony failed, most of the gifted French settlers moved to nearby Dallas. The highly developed skills of these well-educated authors, scientists, artists, musicians, and others brought to frontier Dallas a cultural background that has helped to make the city what it is today.

Swedish settlement was begun at Swedona, and the community retains many of its Swedish customs today.

A colony of the Church of Jesus Christ of Latter-Day Saints (Mormons) set up a settlement called Zodiac. When this first settlement was damaged by floods, they set up a new community called Mormon Mill. The name had an interesting origin. The wonderful millstone they had imported from France had been lost in the flood. Their leader, Lyman Wight, fasted for three days and prayed to find the stone. He then led a party directly to a pile of sand, where they found the missing millstone under 4 feet (about 1.2 meters) of sand. The colonists considered this a miracle. The mill which they set up was used by settlers up to two days' journey away.

No discussion of the influence of various nationalities can overlook the vast contributions to Texas life and culture made by the Spanish and Mexicans. Many of these, of course, can trace their family histories in Texas back many generations. The feast days, festivals, and celebrations were happy contributions of the Latin people to the state.

After joining the United States, Texas claimed a much larger area than that included in the present boundaries. In the compromise of 1850, Congress offered Texas ten million dollars to give up its claim to parts of Oklahoma, Kansas, Wyoming, Colorado, and New Mexico. With the money, the state paid its debt, and used two million to set up a permanent school fund.

ANOTHER FLAG FLIES

The argument between North and South over slavery grew in intensity. With the hope that he could help keep Texas in the Union, Sam Houston ran for governor in 1859, and won.

Few prophets have ever shown greater foresight than Governor Houston when he wrote: "I cannot for a moment entertain the belief that any cause for secession or disunion exists, or that the masses of the people would be willing to precipitate the country into all the horrors of revolution and civil war. If madness and fanaticism should so far prevail as to bring about this disastrous state of affairs, no human being could calculate the injury that would be inflicted upon mankind."

In spite of his warnings, on January 28, 1861, Sam Houston lost his last great fight. A Texas convention voted to secede from the Union, and the people ratified this move in February. Texas had been a state for only fifteen years. In view of the unique circumstance under which Texas joined the Union, it would appear that she might have had a much better legal right to withdraw than some of the other states.

However, Sam Houston would not agree to this. He refused to swear allegiance to the Confederate States, and was deposed as governor. He retired to his home, a tired and defeated old man.

The new governor, Edward Clark, had to mobilize for war.

During the war, the principal battles in Texas were those of Sabine Pass and the Union capture of Galveston, with its recapture by Confederate forces, which held it until the end of the war.

The Federal fleet maintained a blockade of Texas ports, and Corpus Christi was captured. Most of Texas remained out of Union hands, and the Battle of Mansfield was the last major northern attempt to take Texas. Murderous raids by the Indians were experienced during the war years.

One of the great contributions of Texas to the war was its ability to supply huge amounts of materials from the outside world by way of Mexico. Brownsville was one of the principal ports of the South. Called the Backdoor of the Confederacy, its supply lines were never cut off during the war. Vast economic aid went out from Texas to the rest of the Confederate States.

An example of the determination of Texas in providing supplies is the cartridge and percussion cap factory set up in the chambers of the Supreme Court building at Austin. All of its machinery was homemade.

During the war, 60,000 Texans fought for the Confederacy, and nearly 2,000 for the Union. One of the most famous outfits was the Texas Brigade of General John B. Hood.

The last battle of the war was fought at Palmito Hill near Brownsville. Strangely enough, this battle occurred more than a month after Lee had surrendered at Appomattox. Confederate troops had not yet heard that the war was over, and so the last shot of the conflict was fired on Texas soil.

After the war was over, the unsurrendered forces commanded by General Joseph O. Shelby crossed the Rio Grande River into Mexico on July 4, 1865. The troops paused in mid-stream, lowered the last, unsurrendered Confederate flag into the river, and cast a defiant plume into the water before crossing to the other side.

One of the strangest facts of the war concerns Marshall, Texas. For some time this Texas town served as the capital of Missouri, after the governor of Missouri had fled there to escape capture and to set up his government in exile.

A DISORGANIZED SOCIETY

At the close of the war, conditions had become almost intolerable. Even before the war ended, Governor Pendleton Murrah, who was very ill, said in a speech, "In some sections society is almost disorganized . . . murder, robbery, outrages of every kind."

When General Joe Shelby passed through on his way to Mexico, Governor Murrah joined him. Later Shelby related the tragic scene: "He knew death was near to him, yet he put on his old gray uniform, mounted his old war horse and rode away, dying in Mexico."

President Andrew Johnson appointed Andrew J. Hamilton to govern Texas. Later the entire South was placed under military rule, with Texas under the command of General Philip H. Sheridan. The period that followed was full of heartaches, as the so-called carpetbaggers and scalawags attempted to promote their own interests with little concern for the welfare of the people.

On March 30, 1870, Texas was readmitted to the Union. At that time, Texas' Republican governor, Edmund J. Davis, was ruling as a dictator. When Davis ran again for governor in 1873, he was defeated by Richard Coke, but Davis refused to accept the defeat. He remained in his office on the first floor with a guard, while Coke and the legislature held the second floor, also with armed guards. President Grant refused to help Davis; Governor Coke took over, and the most troubled period in Texas history came to an end.

Governor Coke proclaimed: "Let the hearts of the people throb with joy, for the old landmarks of constitutional representative government, so long lost, are this day restored, and the ancient liberties of the people of Texas re-established."

A new constitution became the law of Texas on February 15, 1876, and with amendments, this is still the basic law of the state.

WEALTH ON THE HOOF

During the war, the number of longhorns increased until Texas almost seemed overrun with them. Most Texans thought the beef tough and of little value, but the East needed cattle. With the nearest railroads far away, there seemed little prospect of getting large numbers of cattle to market.

Then in 1867 the first Texas cattle were driven over a route first traveled by Jesse Chisholm from Texas to Abilene, Kansas, where the railroad then ended. In less than six months after the first drive, 35,000 longhorns were driven up the long, dusty Chisholm Trail to Abilene. As the rail lines moved closer to Texas, other towns became the shipping points for cattle. Dodge City, Kansas, was the most famous. In the years 1870 to 1890 an incredible ten million cattle, with their spreading horns were moved from Texas. The two hundred million dollars this brought in helped to rebuild the state and gave Texas its first great business.

A more peaceful current scene as cattlemen drive longhorn steers through Lubbock to a corral at the Ranching Heritage Center during the Bicentennial.

The dashing success with which Texas cowboys met the problems of moving 3,000 cattle in a single herd which stretched out over several miles, and protecting them from danger and stampede, gave the Texans a reputation for toughness and daring. No other industry has ever been quite so picturesque. New towns, new customs, and a distinct new type of people sprang from cattle drives.

A tough job demanded strong, tough people, and the Wild West came into its own. When the railroad conductor called one town, he would bellow, "Cotulla; get your guns ready." Feuds, local wars, notorious gunmen—all took their places in the legends of the West.

The first day Wyatt Earp, a noted lawman, was in El Paso, he saw two men shot to death in the same room within thirty minutes. He never came back to El Paso. One of the most feared gunmen was John Wesley Hardin, who was killed by El Paso constable and gun slinger John Selman. Selman died in another gunfight a few months later.

Just as the West came to mean much that was violent and lawless, the name of the Texas Rangers has come to stand for law and order in a gallant manner. One of the most interesting and unusual stories of the Rangers is the roundup at Junction in 1877.

The number of outlaws in Kimble County had become more than the Rangers could control. They decided to apply the tactics of the cattle country to the problem, and ordered every man in the county rounded up in a mesquite flat just outside of Junction. When their roundup was finished, they were able to take out the men they wanted—horse thieves, robbers, cattle thieves, outlaws, murderers. Since there was no jail, they were chained to trees. The innocent were released.

In the end, the greatest tamer of the Wild West was a simple twist of metal. Barbed wire was invented in 1874, and from that time the range was never quite the same. Ranchers, who had used the land as they saw fit, took up arms against the fencing of the range. There were innumerable barbed-wire wars, but fencing gradually won out. In 1874 the almost unbelievable area of 3,050,000 acres (about 1,200,000 hectares) of the XIT ranch was fenced, as were hundreds more.

A GROWING STATE

The Texas State Fair was founded in 1886. Texas claimed the first quadruplets ever born in America—a surprise 1890 addition to the Page family of Redwater.

Theodore Roosevelt and Colonel Leonard Wood were in San Antonio recruiting Rough Riders at the start of the Spanish-American War, and training them at the fairgrounds. Their accomplishments in the war were to make them famous.

As the century drew to a close, the Brazo River flooded, killing thirty persons and causing nine million dollars damage. A year later, in 1900, Nature brought far worse destruction.

A mighty hurricane swept across the Gulf of Mexico, and hit Galveston with winds up to 110 miles (about 177 kilometers) per hour. Mountainous waves dashed over the low-lying city. The destruction and loss of life made this the worst natural disaster ever to strike the United States. Although no exact figures are known, at least 6,000 people were killed, and 8,000 made homeless. Property damage totaled thirty million dollars. The force of the storm can be illustrated by the 4,000 ton (about 3,630 metric tons) ship which was carried 22 miles (about 35 kilometers) inland from deep water and left stranded there.

The spirit of those who remained was not crushed. A committee immediately was set up to supervise relief, clean-up, and reconstruction. Aid poured in from around the world. Clara Barton, founder of the American Red Cross, supervised Red Cross activities personally. Burial of the bodies was impossible. They were loaded on barges and buried at sea.

Out of this disaster came some progress, however. The committee that had been formed to carry on the emergency work was continued with expanded authority. This was the beginning of a plan devised by Galveston to govern the city by a commission. This pioneer Galveston plan has been widely adopted by other cities.

The people of Galveston were determined that no such disaster would overtake them again. They raised the level of the city 8 feet (about 2.4 meters) and built a heavy 16 foot (about 4.8 meters)

The Lyndon Baines Johnson Space Center in Houston.

seawall as a barrier for the ocean. The hurricane of 1915 showed how well their plan was carried out. The city was spared, although the force of the storm was so great that it hurled a three-masted schooner high over the seawall into Fort Crockett.

In 1901 an earth-shaking roar was followed by a stupendous flow of oil at Beaumont's Spindletop well. This was the beginning of the oil industry.

In 1910 Texas witnessed a pioneer military event of far-reaching effects. In that year at San Antonio, Lieutenant Benjamin D. Foulois unpacked what looked like a crate of bamboo poles with an engine attached. That one man and one machine formed the United States Air Force.

Congress had purchased the wrecked secondhand plane from the Wright brothers. The Air Force budget was $150, and Lieutenant Foulois spent $300 of his own money to fix up the plane. He had studied with the Wrights to learn what little was then known about flying. After some hair-raising experiences in the skies of Texas, Lieutenant Foulois managed to get the U.S. Air Force operating in good style. At San Antonio he made a number of inventions contributing to aviation. He was the inventor of wheels on airplanes. Before, they had been on skids. He also devised the first safety belts.

In 1915 and 1916 unsettled times in Mexico caused raids across

46

the boundary and serious disturbances. The National Guard was mobilized along the Texas border, and General John Pershing led an expedition into Mexico.

In the year 1917, Texas rocked with charges about misuse of funds, and improper treatment of the university. This brought about the impeachment and removal from office of Governor James E. Ferguson.

In 1917, the young men of Texas were called to enter the service of their country. More than 200,000 Texans served in the armed forces during World War I.

A Texan, "Colonel" E.M. House, became one of the leading national political figures as advisor to President Woodrow Wilson. He was often referred to as assistant president.

TRIALS AND TRIUMPHS

Once again Texas proved its leadership in petroleum with the discovery in 1931 of another of the world's great oil fields—this time at Longview.

The Texas Centennial Exposition at Dallas in 1936 celebrated the one-hundredth anniversary of Texas independence, and left to the State Fairgrounds a number of its finest buildings as a permanent legacy of this exposition.

In 1937 Texas and the world were shocked and grieved at the worst disaster of its kind when a school explosion in New London brought violent death to 279 pupils, two teachers, and two visitors.

During World War II, 23,022 Texans died. Texans in the armed services totaled 750,000.

Thirty Texans received the Congressional Medal of Honor for their extraordinary services during World War II. Texas provided 155 generals and twelve admirals.

The weather and other natural advantages of the state made Texas a leading center of war training. Corpus Christi was the site of the world's largest naval air-training base. The wide reaches of Texas also contained twenty-one prisoner-of-war camps during the war.

In 1953 the long-fought tidelands oil dispute was settled in favor of the tideland states. Texas added 1,878,000 acres (about 760,000 hectares) of offshore lands to its total area as a result of this decision.

In 1961 Houston became the command post for the nation's space projects. The Manned Spacecraft Center on Clear Lake, completed in 1964, makes that city the space capital of the world.

San Antonio helps to maintain Texas' space lead with the world's first Aerospace Medical Center. Here leading scientists study the effects of oxygen, pressures, temperatures, and other space-travel hazards on the human body.

A dispute with Mexico was solved in 1963. Mexico had claimed 437 acres (about 177 hectares) of El Paso in a section called El Chamizal. The dispute came about because of a shift in the Rio Grande. An arbitration committee had awarded the area to Mexico, but the United States refused to recognize this. The 1963 agreement transferred a sizeable chunk of El Paso to the Mexican side, with U.S. property owners receiving payment for their property.

TRAGEDY!

On November 22, 1963, the world's eyes turned to Dallas. John Fitzgerald Kennedy, thirty-fifth President of the United States, was visiting Dallas, acknowledging the cheers of a large and enthusiastic crowd as he rode through the streets in an open car. Suddenly shots rang out, and horrified spectators saw the President slump limply in his seat. The governor of Texas, John B. Connally, Jr., was severely wounded by one of the shots. Although the President was rushed to Parkland Hospital, he never recovered consciousness.

Only a few minutes after the assassination, a Texan, Vice-President Lyndon Baines Johnson, received the oath of office as President of the United States. Johnson served as President until January, 1969, and he died January 22, 1973.

Today Texas holds a high place in every aspect of American life, ranking among the top five states in size, mineral production, population, and agriculture, and sixth in manufacturing.

Natural Treasures

BIRDS, BEES, AND BEASTS

One of the world's great dramas in natural history has been unfolding in Texas. A little group of birds on the Aransas Wildlife Refuge north of Corpus Christi gets more publicity than many kings and heads of countries. These, of course, are the world's last of the huge and beautiful whooping cranes. Only a few of these wonderful creatures still remain, and except for a few in zoos and controlled areas, all of these birds winter in Aransas. People everywhere follow their annual migrations to Canada and back with tremendous interest to see if all the older birds are still alive, and to count any young members added during the summer.

Another Texas bird of distinction is the rare Colima warbler of the Big Bend region. However, there is no general scarcity of birds in Texas. There have been more than a thousand varieties recognized in the state, from the coastal wading and swimming birds to feathered inhabitants of the dry cactus country. One unusual Texas treasure is its wealth of wild turkeys. Almost half of the wild turkeys remaining in the United States are in Texas.

One state inhabitant whose population used to number hundreds of millions is now also vanishing. This is the prairie dog, which has been almost exterminated. Many zoos have attempted to preserve them in living exhibits such as the Prairie Dog Town at Lubbock. Another almost vanished Texan is the great gray wolf. However, his cousin the coyote is so wily that he continues in great numbers in spite of constant effort to exterminate him.

Texas has one of the largest reptile populations in the country, including alligators in the semi-tropical areas. Mountain lions and jaguarundi, peccaries (javelina or wild pig), armadillo, antelope, deer, bear, and even the last herd of bighorn sheep in Texas in the Diablo Mountains, give variety to the state's wildlife population.

The great herds of buffaloes and wild mustangs are no longer found. Like wild cattle, tremendous herds of wild horses were

Right: Coastal birds have settled on an island formed as a dredging disposal area (below) near Corpus Christi.

rounded up and sent to Eastern markets. Various horses among the mustang herds became famous. The best known of these, perhaps, was Midnight, who became almost a legend because of his ability to keep his herd away from danger.

Even some Texas bees have an unusual reputation. The bees in the region around Uvalde gather nectar from special desert blossoms of the region, and create the unique Uvalde Honey, of world-wide fame.

More than 250 species of fish are found along 3,359 miles (about 5,406 kilometers) of Gulf coastal waters, in Texas' many lakes, and in the rivers. Sport fishermen find almost every type of fishing from deep-sea fishing for marlin to angling for the channel catfish of the Rio Grande, which grow to unusual size. Oysters and shrimp also provide seafood lovers with many a tasty morsel.

ROOTED IN TEXAS

There are about 24,000,000 acres (about 10,000,000 hectares) of timber in Texas, a land generally thought of as open prairie. Four national forests are established within the state. Most important of the forest areas is the Piney Woods region.

A most unique Texas forest area, about 2,000,000 acres (about 800,000 hectares), is the Big Thicket. This is a jungle of trees and undergrowth, in some places so thick it cannot be penetrated. It is unusual because it is not swampy as most similar areas are.

Another unusual woodland area in Texas is the Lost Pines of Bastrop. This group of trees is completely isolated from the pine forests of east Texas. Still another oddity, the tiny shin oak in west Texas, grows to a height of only 12 to 18 inches (about 30 to 46 centimeters). A species of juniper in the Big Bend area is found nowhere else in the world.

Arizona cypress, Douglas fir, ponderosa pine, and quaking aspen are found in Texas. It is the only state where both the Rocky Mountain trees and the eastern oaks and pines are native. Exotic fruit trees such as citrus and papaya have been brought in. The beautiful springtime dogwood trails of Texas are a noted tourist attraction.

In keeping with its reputation for bigness, Texas lists eight trees as being the largest of their type in the country, including the country's largest American holly tree.

More wildflowers grow in Texas than in any other state, according to botanists. There are 5,000 varieties of native wildflowers in the state. Five hundred seventy different species of grass are native to Texas.

Texas delights the nature lover with every type of bloom from the breathtaking loveliness of vast reaches of desert cactus in bloom to tropical plants like the oleander lining the streets of Galveston, and the enormous poinsettias and vast mounds of striking bougainvillea. A wisteria vine at Fern Lake Ranch near Camp Wood has a main stem 4 feet (about 1.2 meters) in circumference.

The mysterious Big Thicket breeds many exotic plants, including as many as fifteen varieties of orchids. Rare ferns grow 6 feet (about 1.8 meters) tall. The Big Thicket is one of the country's few remaining areas still almost untouched by human hands.

Big-leaved caladium lines the banks of the Comal River. Some of the lovely desert flowers, including orchids, maguey, sotol, in addition to cacti, all grow in such areas as the Davis Mountains.

An interesting weed, the candelila, provides a high-quality wax that is used in many ways.

The red wolf, an endangered species.

Now the Big Thicket Preserve can be visited in style.

MINERAL WEALTH

Nature has given Texas great mineral wealth. The value of petroleum reserves alone in Texas is greater than the value of the total known mineral reserves in any other state except Alaska.

Texas has the fantastic total of almost one third of all the known underground oil reserves in the United States!

Sulphur, natural gas, salt, silver, mercury, helium, graphite, zinc, copper, lead, manganese, gold, and gypsum—all are found in Texas.

Right: The oil "boom" began with the Lucas gusher as shown in an actual photo from January 10, 1901. Its enormous spouting continued for nine days until it was finally capped. Today (below) a modern monument at Beaumont marks the historic event.

The People Use Their Treasures

MIDAS WAS A PIKER

Texas is far and away the leading mineral producing state. The total value of its mineral production sometimes exceeds one fourth of the entire U.S. production. The value of annual mineral production in the mid-1970s was over $16,000,000,000. Of this, close to ten billion came from petroleum alone.

The Anthony F. Lucas well in the Spindletop field near Beaumont threw its pipe into the air in 1901 and spouted a flow of oil upward for 200 feet (about 60 meters). This was the discovery well of the Texas oil industry. Before the Lucas well could be controlled, it had created an oily lake covering 100 acres (about 40 hectares). The Lucas well was the first of the salt dome discoveries.

The boom which came to Beaumont after Spindletop was much larger, rougher, and tougher than that of most gold or silver mining camps.

A smaller well at Corsicana in 1894 was the first commercial oil well in Texas. The first rotary drilling rig was also developed and built there.

Other oil discoveries followed—Ranger, East Texas (biggest of them all), Permian, and others. Oil exploration continues strong in Texas today. By the mid-1970s, the number of producing wells had declined, but still exceeded 160,000.

Texas is the world's largest producer of sulphur. The Spindletop pioneer, A.F. Lucas, was also the discoverer of Texas sulphur.

Today's demand for natural gas and the dwindling U.S. supplies make Texas' resources more important. Almost one third of all proved reserves of natural gas in the United States—79 trillion cubic feet (about 2.2 trillion cubic meters)—are in Texas.

Texas is also one of the great helium states, and it leads the country in asphalt production. The world's largest antimony smelter is at Laredo.

Next to petroleum and natural gas, cement is the largest of Texas' mineral industries.

MANUFACTURING

Texas' refineries in the Houston-Beaumont-Gulf area account for almost one third of the total United States refining capacity, putting Texas well in front in this vital industry.

The total value of general Texas chemicals now exceeds a billion dollars per year, making chemicals the biggest single industry in the state, and the only one of a billion-dollar value. A large part of Texas chemicals is manufactured from petroleum. These are called petrochemicals. In this field, half of all U.S. synthetic rubber is produced in Texas, the country's leader in artificial rubber.

The Ethyl-Dow Chemical plant at Freeport is one of Texas' largest manufacturers and is the nation's largest producer of chemicals from seawater. Complicated processes extract magnesium and bromines.

Altogether, Texas' manufacturing plants add over eighteen billion dollars to the state each year, making Texas sixth among the states in manufacturing.

Dramatic advances have been made in electronics, with the Texas Instruments Plant at Dallas as an example, and also in aluminum. Fort Worth is one of the largest aircraft production centers in America.

Much heavy industry has come to the Gulf Coast as well as to such communities as Longview, with its great Le Tourneau earthmoving equipment plant. Dallas leads the world in the production of cotton gin machinery.

Although not of great commercial importance, one of the unique industries in the world is claimed by Monahans. The type of desert fleas which grow there are the best for flea circuses, and so Monahans is the center for the capture of these athletic circus animals.

FARM AND FIELD

A growing percentage of Texas people now live in urban areas, but the state still has more acres of crops harvested every year than any

A cotton picker at work in the fields.

other. Texas ranks first in the production of cotton, cottonseed, sorghum grain, rice, and cowpeas (black-eyed peas).

In livestock, Texas ranks number one in all cattle, beef cattle, sheep and wool, and goats. The total value of farm products each year is close to six billion dollars.

Texas remains the foremost cowboy and cattle empire. In 1874 the native longhorns were mixed with Brahman cattle from India. This resulted in a type of cattle which was immune to tick fever and provided better beef.

James Taylor White was the first modern Anglo-American rancher.

Today there are many large ranches in the state, but the best-known probably is the great 865,000 acre (about 350,000 hectares) King Ranch, at Kingsville. At the ranch, King's son-in-law, Robert Kleburg, developed the only distinct, true breed of cattle ever produced in the United States—the Santa Gertrudis.

Now ranches are modern in every way. Even the hated prickly pear has been tamed. A prickly pear burner now flames away the spines of this tough plant. The wise old cattle come running when they hear the burner, because they know they will soon be able to feast on this despined delicacy.

One of the many legends of the cattle industry tells of the great

Paul Bunyan who built an enormous pipeline to carry his cattle to market, just as lesser beings do for their petroleum and natural gas. However, Paul had to give his pipeline up, the story goes, because the threads that held the joints together were so big that the cattle kept getting caught in them.

Half of the world's supply of mohair is produced in Texas, and this is 97 percent of all U.S. mohair, which is produced by angora goats. The greatest centers for goats are San Angelo and Uvalde. At Roosevelt, after sheep are sheared, they wear shirts, and goats wear coats to protect them and keep them warm. Karakul Sheep Ranch near Holliday is the largest of its type. These fur sheep were obtained by Theodore Roosevelt from the Czar of Russia.

Long before the cattle industry came, however, Texas was an agricultural area. Jared Grose is called the father of Texas agriculture. He grew the first commercial cotton, and used a cotton gin. East Texas, like the southern states, grows cotton, sugar cane, and rice. Jefferson County is the heart of the rice-growing area.

Egyptian long-staple cotton is grown near Ysleta. Regular and "winter" vegetables add to the prosperity of Laredo and Brownsville. The Rio Grande region is the oldest irrigated area of the United States. Citrus—oranges, lemons, limes, and the delicious ruby-red grapefruit—are all fine products of the lower Rio Grande valley.

Tyler is known as the rose garden of the world. More than half of the field roses of the United States grow there.

Texas holds almost a monopoly on mohair from angora goats.

Shearing sheep.

TRANSPORTATION AND COMMUNICATION

At one time Texas had no deep-water ports, yet today the state is one of the leaders in tonnage of ocean shipping. In the mid-1970s the state moved a total of nearly 250,000,000 tons (about 227,000,000 metric tons) of goods annually. Houston is third in tonnage among U.S. ocean ports.

Texas is the only state with five of the major ports of the United States—Houston, Beaumont, Port Arthur, Corpus Christi, and Texas City—in the order of their volume. Altogether there are thirteen deep-water ports in Texas. All of these have had to be improved by dredging and other means.

The most important waterways are the Houston Ship Channel, 300 feet (about 91 meters) wide, 36 feet (about 11 meters) deep, and 50 miles (about 80 kilometers) long; the Sabine-Neches Waterway; and the Intracoastal Canal.

The first railroad in Texas was the Buffalo Bayou, Brazos and Colorado. It began operations in 1853. In that same year, Texas made its first land grant to encourage railroad building. Texas was unique among all the states because in the statehood agreement it reserved all of its public lands for the state. In other states most public lands were in the hands of the federal government. In all, Texas gave more than 38,000 square miles (about 98,000 square kilometers) of public land for railroad building. This is an area larger than the state of Indiana.

One of the most interesting stories in railroad history was the desperate struggle to bring the first railroad to Fort Worth. The Texas and Pacific was stalled by lack of funds before it reached the city. The people of Fort Worth offered to grade the remaining roadbed in order to get the road to the city. This had to be done, however,

The busy Intracoastal waterway.

before the legislature adjourned, or the railroad's land grant would be lost. Almost all the men of Fort Worth went to work grading or laying track, while the women fed the workers and the mules. Just in time, the first locomotive pulled into Fort Worth on July 19, 1876, with the local newspaper editor stoking the boiler.

Texas has the most miles of improved highway in the country. Also there are more miles of interstate highways than in any other state. This is a far cry from the Central National Road of the Republic of Texas. Its major advantage was the fact that the builders were forbidden to leave tree stumps more than 12 inches (about 30 centimeters) high in the middle of the road.

El Camino del Rio, along the Rio Grande in the Big Bend area, is one of the nation's most beautiful highways.

In 1870, Waco had the longest suspension bridge in the United States—a span of 475 feet (about 145 meters). Cattle hoofs once thundered across it on their way over the Brazos. Today the Southern Pacific crosses the Pecos River on one of the highest railroad bridges in the world, the Pecos High Bridge. The Pecos Highway 90 bridge is the highest highway bridge in the Southwest.

One of the great projects of its type was the Houston-New York pipeline. More miles of pipeline for oil and gas originate in Texas than anywhere else in the country.

The Spanish *Gaceta de Texas,* published in 1813, was the first newspaper in the state, but the first significant newspaper of lasting importance was the San Felipe *Telegraph and Texas Register,* begun in 1835. The first radio station in Texas was WRR, owned by the city of Dallas.

RIGHT IN STYLE

Retail trade in Texas each year exceeds thirty billion dollars. Leading the list of Texas retail stores is one of the world's best-known and most highly respected merchandising establishments—Neiman-Marcus of Dallas. Dallas has become known as a style-setter in women's clothing, and Dallas fashions are highly regarded.

Right: A portrait of Lyndon B. Johnson by David Philip Wilson. Below: The Lyndon B. Johnson Library at the University of Texas, Austin, is the first Presidential library to be established at a university. Its collections total a mammoth 31,000,000 items and many fascinating displays.

Human Treasures

SAM HOUSTON

The life of Sam Houston was one of the most unusual and dramatic among all of the best-known names of the country. He served twice as president of a country, was governor of two different states, ambassador of the Cherokee Indians, United States congressman, and senator. He was born in Virginia, near Lexington, March 2, 1793. When he was fourteen, he ran away to live with the Indians. "There I was initiated into the profound mysteries of the red man's character," he wrote. He became the adopted son of Cherokee Chief Oo-loo-te-ka. He did not cut himself off from his family completely, but returned whenever he wanted a favor from them.

Later he joined the army and became a hero for his bravery under the command of Andrew Jackson. Then he studied law, became a congressman from Tennessee, and finally, with the backing of his powerful friend, Andrew Jackson, Sam Houston became governor of Tennessee.

He married, but very soon after was separated from his wife. The reasons for this personal tragedy have never been revealed. In disgrace, he resigned the governorship, and fled to his friends the Cherokee, then living in Arkansas. A promising career of a brilliant and charming man appeared to be ruined.

Houston sank into such depths that he was sometimes known as the "Big Drunk." In spite of this, he helped prevent an Indian war, and became a Cherokee citizen. They sent him to Washington as their ambassador, where he created a sensation by dressing in the most flamboyant Indian clothes, with a different bright blanket and a fresh feather for his head every day. Or he might wear his famous leopard-skin vest. His friend Andrew Jackson invited him to the White House. Just what plans they hatched there no one knows.

Some writers say that both Jackson and Houston had long intended to free Texas from the Mexicans, although Houston had never been in Texas. When he finally did go to Texas, apparently he had no very clear course of action in mind.

The most remarkable thing about Sam Houston is that when opportunity came his way he not only made the most of it and led the Texans to victory, but he also continued from that point on as a man of great and noble character.

As president of the Texas Republic he governed well and justly, bringing order out of chaos. It is notable that he had the respect of the Indians. During his term no Indian tribe violated its treaty.

In his second term as president of the Texas Republic, at a very critical time, he had to undo the mistakes of his predecessor.

Later, as a Texas senator, he spent ten years vigorously opposing any thought of southern withdrawal from the Union. There are some experts who say he might have become president if he had been less devoted to principle.

Later, as governor of Texas, he continued as a lonely Southern fighter against the tide sweeping toward secession. He died at Huntsville on July 26, 1863, an impoverished old man, given little honor by the state and country he served so long and well.

Some of his best thoughts occur in a speech he made just after being forced from the governorship of Texas for not taking an oath to uphold the Confederacy: "I protest against surrendering the Federal Constitution, its government and its glorious flag to the Northern Abolition leaders and to accept in its stead a so-called Confederate Government whose constitution contains the germs and seeds of decay which must and will lead to its speedy ruin. . . . When the tug of war comes . . . the fearful conflict will fill our fair land with untold suffering, misfortune and disaster. The soil of our beloved South will drink deep the precious blood of our sons and brethren. . . . The die has been cast by your secession leaders, whom you have permitted to sow and broadcast the seeds of secession, and you must before long reap the fearful harvest of conspiracy and revolution."

MR. PRESIDENT

Two presidents of the United States were natives of Texas. Dwight

The Lyndon B. Johnson Home.

David Eisenhower was born October 14, 1890, in Denison, Texas. However, his parents moved to Kansas when Dwight was only a year old, and the well-loved general-statesman did not live in Texas after that, except for a short assignment at Fort Sam Houston after his graduation from West Point.

Lyndon Johnson was born on a farm near Stonewall, Texas, August 27, 1908. He worked his way through college, became a teacher, then went into politics. President Franklin D. Roosevelt named him as Texas administrator of the National Youth Administration. He won a seat in Congress, and with the coming of World War II he went to the Pacific front where he won a Silver Star for a daring flight over New Guinea.

In 1948 Johnson ran for the Senate, and won the office by a margin of only 87 votes, the narrowest margin in Texas history. However, once elected, his success as a senator was so great that he won re-election overwhelmingly, and later, at the age of forty-four, became the Democratic leader in the Senate. His power and influence soared, and he became known as the second-most-powerful man in Washington.

He sought unsuccessfully the Democratic nomination for president in 1956 and 1960. In 1960, John F. Kennedy asked Mr. Johnson to become the candidate for vice-president, and he accepted. On the death of President Kennedy, Lyndon Baines Johnson inherited the position he had wanted so much. About this sad inheritance he said, "All I have I would have given gladly not to be standing here today."

OTHER PUBLIC FIGURES

Besides Lyndon Johnson, another Texan has been vice-president of the United States. This was John Nance Garner, native of Detroit, Texas, who returned to his home at Uvalde after serving under President Franklin D. Roosevelt.

The man who is known as The Father of Texas is Stephen Austin. When his father, Moses Austin, died, he asked Stephen to carry on his (Moses') work of creating an American settlement in Texas. As one writer has said, "Stephen Austin did carry on with it, and in so doing managed to erect for his father and for himself a magnificent monument. That monument is the state of Texas."

The most successful husband and wife team to serve as governors of a state are Miriam A. and James E. Ferguson. "Ma" Ferguson became one of the first women to serve as governors. Both she and Nellie Tayloe Ross of Wyoming were elected on the same day. Mrs. Ferguson ran to avenge her husband who had been removed from office and could not serve again. When someone said her husband would probably run the office behind the scenes, she replied, "This way you get two governors for the price of one."

Another husband and wife team in Texas public affairs consisted of Oveta Culp Hobby and William P. Hobby; he was governor of Texas from 1917 to 1921. Mrs. Hobby became the first woman to wear an army uniform, as head of the Women's Army Corps during World War II. Later she gained even greater fame as the first Secretary of Health, Education and Welfare, under President Eisenhower.

James Stephen Hogg, one of Texas' best governors, was the first native of Texas ever elected to the governor's chair.

One of Texas' most distinguished public servants was long-time speaker of the House of Representatives, Sam Rayburn, who was for many years one of the nation's most influential men.

HEROES ALL

Outstanding in the eyes of all Texans, and perhaps even in all the world, is the fame of the little band of heroes who died in the Alamo, fighting to make Texas free.

The most prominent of them had gained nationwide fame as men of action. The exploits of Davy Crockett are known to every lover of westerns. Almost equally well known was James Bowie, inventor of the knife which still bears his name. He loved excitement and adventure. His brother said that Jim liked nothing better than to rope and ride alligators, and that he once fought a knife duel with three men, killing two and wounding the third. His reputation soared even higher when he was supposed to have found the fabulous, legendary, lost San Saba gold mine.

James Butler Bonham deserves a special kind of respect from patriotic Texans. In order to get to Texas, to fight and die with his friend Colonel Travis, Bonham had to borrow the money for the trip. During the siege of the Alamo he left the mission building to try to get help, but he returned, knowing it was certain death.

In the words of the Alamo Cenotaph, these comrades in the Alamo, "chose never to surrender nor retreat. These brave hearts with flag still proudly waving perished in the flames of immortality that their high sacrifice might lead to the founding of this Texas."

Mention must also be made of the long fight by Mrs. Clara Driscoll Fevier to preserve the Alamo as a shrine.

CULTURE ON THE PLAINS

In the years when the cold war with Russia seemed to be going badly for the United States, when Americans were little-known in many parts of the world for their cultural achievements, a remarkable event took place. A young Texas concert pianist won the greatest international artistic prize of the Soviet Union—the Tschaikovsky Award. This was Van Cliburn, of Kilgore, who became a hero in the arts, acclaimed around the world. His achievement is said to have done as much to help American and Soviet good will as any other single incident.

Two unusual women artists have brought Texas renown in paint-

Davy Crocket painted by William Henry Huddle.

ing and sculpture. Eugenie Lavender had known the luxury of the French court under Louis Napoleon. When she and her husband came to Texas in 1851, they endured the hard life of pioneers. He was held captive for a while by the Indians. Together they killed rattlesnakes and put out prairie fires. When her supply of paint was gone, she made her own from clay, herbs, leaves, and flowers, and she persisted in an outstanding career in painting.

Elizabet Ney had won fame as a sculptress in Europe. She was a friend of the great musicians and artists there. She and her husband came to the Texas wilderness in 1870. She offered, in her home, the first formal art instruction in Texas. Her sculpture was famous throughout the world. She did the statues of Sam Houston and Stephen Austin for the Hall of Fame in the national Capitol.

Writer George Sessions Perry of Rockdale, world famous portrait painter Douglas Chandor of Weatherford, and Frank Van der Stucken, composer and conductor, of Fredericksburg, are other Texas artists.

To the list of Texas immortals should be added the names of Harold Morris and Radie Britain, composers; J. Frank Dobie and Katherine Anne Porter, authors; and Walter Prescott Webb, one of America's outstanding historians of the West.

SUCH INTERESTING PEOPLE

Richard King and Miffling Kenedy began their careers in Texas as the owners and captains of a Rio Grande steamboat. They made a fortune blockade running during the Civil War, and used the money to create the famous King Ranch. Ranches brought wealth and fame in a different way to John Warne "Bet-a-Million" Gates. He set up his barbed wire fence in a city plaza in San Antonio and proved to the skeptical cattlemen that it would hold the toughest cattle. He made a large fortune and was later associated with Arthur Edward Stillwell in building Port Arthur. Stillwell claimed that the plan for Port Arthur had come to him from the spirit world.

On a trip to Fort Worth, Indian Chiefs Yellow Bear and Quanah Parker stayed in a hotel. They had never seen gas lights before. When they went to bed, they blew the lights out. Yellow Bear died of gas asphyxiation, but Parker recovered and became a good friend of the settlers. When he learned that the town of Quanah had been named for him, he said: "May the Great Spirit smile on you, town. May the rains fall in due season; and in the warmth of the sunshine after the rain, may the earth yield bountifully. May peace and contentment dwell with you and your children forever."

Gail Borden, Texas pioneer, was the inventor of condensed milk and founder of the Borden company. Borden County and the town of Gail are named for him. Jesse Holman Jones is known as the principal builder of the modern city of Houston. Admiral Chester W. Nimitz of World War II fame was born in Fredericksburg.

Hall of Fame baseball players Tris Speaker and Rogers Hornsby were Texas men. In another field of sport, Jack Johnson of Galveston knocked out Jim Jeffries at Reno, Nevada, to win the world heavyweight boxing championship. He gained his strength on the Galveston docks, lifting 500-pound (about 227-kilogram) bales of cotton.

Jules Bledsoe became nationally famous for his singing of the song *Ol' Man River* in the musical *Show Boat.*

George Wilkins Kendall of Boerne has been called the first modern war correspondent. Wartime fame came also to Audie Murphy of Farmersville. He earned more decorations during World War II than any other person, and is considered the outstanding individual hero of that war.

The University of Texas tower and Littlefield Fountain.

Teaching and Learning

When the Republic of Texas in 1839 set aside fifty leagues of land to establish two universities, no one imagined that this would assure the creation of one of the wealthiest university on the face of the earth. The University of Texas was opened at Austin in 1883. In 1923 oil was found on the university land, and its current endowment is said to rank with that of Harvard University as the largest in the country. Its main plant was built entirely without tax funds.

The university is a member of the Association of American Universities, which includes the 50 highest ranked institutions of the country. Faculty now numbers about 2,200 in ten colleges. Its library is particularly famed for its rare book collection.

The Agricultural and Mechanical University of Texas, generally known as Texas A and M, at College Station, has operated since 1876. It has been renowned for its military discipline. Texas Tech and the University of Houston are other major schools. The University of Houston is now state supported.

The first institution of higher education in present-day Texas was Rutersville University, founded at Rutersville in 1840.

Leading schools with religious associations are Hardin-Simmons University at Abilene; St. Edward's University at Austin, sometimes called the Notre Dame of the South; Texas Christian University, Fort Worth; and Southern Methodist University at Dallas.

Rice University, Houston, is famed for its science and engineering schools. Other prominent scientific and technical schools are Texas Technological University, Lubbock; Texas University of Arts and Industry, Kingsville; and Le Tourneau College, Longview. In the field of advanced science, the Science Research Center was established at Dallas as a graduate research center of the Southwest. In agricultural research, the Luling Farm is outstanding.

In all, Texas has more than 150 privately and publicly supported colleges and universities, varying in enrollment from less than 100 to scholastic giants such as the University of Texas with more than 80,000 students.

Texas was one of the early states to establish a free public-school system, which was begun in 1854. However, formal education has been carried on since the days of the Spanish missions. Among other subjects taught in them was music, and these were probably the first music schools in the United States. One of the Franciscan Fathers wrote, "These Indians . . . are today well instrumented and civilized. . . . Many play the harp, the violin, and the guitar well. . . ."

Enchantment of Texas

THE COAST IS CLEAR

When the first European explorers stepped ashore on the shining sandy beaches of Texas, they could hardly have foreseen that those same sandy beaches—32 miles (about 52 kilometers) of them—would be one of the major attractions of a city called Galveston, perched on the eastern end of Galveston Island.

In 1837 a steamboat captain was looking for a town that had just been founded by the Allen brothers only four months after the Battle of San Jacinto, and named for Sam Houston. The community then was so insignificant that the captain passed it by without noticing it. Today Houston is the largest city in Texas, and the sixth or seventh largest city in the United States, depending on which figures you accept.

It is the third greatest port in the United States, and visitors are fascinated by the view of the port from the observation dock. Free sight-seeing trips down the ship canal are available.

Major league baseball came to Houston with the Astros club, and the city determined to build the finest sports stadium in the world. The result was the Harris County Stadium, opened in 1965 at a cost of twenty-four million dollars. It is the first covered stadium suitable for baseball and football, seats 66,000 people under one roof, and is completely air conditioned.

Houston is known for artistic endeavors such as its symphony orchestra. In fact, both Houston and Matagordo had theaters before they had churches. However, there are many fine churches now. The civic center is one of the largest, including Sam Houston Coliseum, Music Hall, and City Auditorium.

Another of the finest of its kind is the vast Texas Medical Center at Houston.

Near Houston is one of the most unusual memorial parks, where the Battle of San Jacinto is commemorated. The mighty monument in memory of the battle where Texas won independence towers 570 feet (about 174 meters) above San Jacinto State Park—higher than the Washington Monument. At its top is a huge star, the emblem of Texas.

A fascinating war memorial is the old battleship *Texas*. Built in 1914, the mighty *Texas* fought in both world wars, and was presented to the people of Texas by the United States Navy. It was permanently moored in the park as a memorial museum.

Not far from Houston is historic San Felipe, where Stephen Austin had his headquarters. Here Austin Memorial Park exhibits a reproduction of Austin's log cabin, and has many other items of interest on the founder of Texas.

One of America's natural treasures, Padre Island, stretches thin and long down the coastline. In order to preserve the priceless, unchanged condition of the island, 88 miles (about 142 kilometers) of the island are a National Seashore Area. Here people may marvel at one of our few unspoiled natural wonders, or perhaps even dig for gold which tradition says the many pirates buried there. Nearby Corpus Christi, built on two levels, and the United States Naval Air Station are other points of interest.

At the opposite end of the coast, in Port Arthur, ships going up and down the Sabine-Neches Waterway seem to be sailing right down the city streets. A particular point of interest in Beaumont is the Temple to the Brave, dedicated to the heroes of all wars in which Texans have had a part.

THE EAST

Huntsville is the site of the unusual home, built like a steamboat, where Sam Houston died. His grave is near the Steamboat House. The Sam Houston Museum in Huntsville offers interesting mementoes of Houston and Mexican President Santa Anna. Huntsville is also the site of the Texas Department of Corrections, formerly the State Penitentiary. The annual Prison Rodeo is a fast-paced benefit for the prisoners' fund, attended by 100,000 people each year.

Crockett, named for Alamo hero Davy Crockett, is one of the few communities to enjoy its trees and make money from them too.

The interior of the Astrodome in Houston.

More than 10,000 pecan trees line the streets, providing shade as well as revenue from the nuts.

Nacogdoches, founded in 1716, has been under eight different flags. It preserves as a museum the old Stone House fort where Sam Houston, James Bowie, Davy Crockett, and Thomas J. Rusk took the oath of allegiance to Texas.

Tyler, center of the nation's field-rose culture, carries on its rose tradition in the Municipal Rose Garden, where there are 30,000 plants in unbelievable profusion. At New London the victims of the terrible school explosion of 1937 are remembered by a memorial sundial, set with a semi-precious stone dedicated to each victim. The region around Marshall is renowned for its very unusual "sacred harp" singing, with each note of the music printed in a different shape. A different scale from that of traditional music is also used.

Mount Pleasant is known for its modern version of medieval jousting, called Riding the Ring, and for its fox hunts. Today only two Indian reservations remain in Texas. The Alabama and Coushata Reservation has a particularly interesting record of peace and progress.

Texas' most northeasterly city, Texarkana, reaches so far to the east that a large part of it spills into Arkansas. To be absolutely impartial, the Federal Building and Post Office and the Union Station straddle the state line, half in one state and half in the other.

75

NORTH-CENTRAL

Dominating much of the financial and cultural life of the state are the two neighboring cities, Dallas and Fort Worth.

Fort Worth has long claimed to be where the West begins, but this is not just a figure of speech. They say that somewhere between Dallas and Fort Worth is the line between East and West. This is literally true. East of Fort Worth are orchards, nurseries, and other evidences of eastern lands. Just beyond its west border, the country stretches out into rolling, treeless plains.

Both Fort Worth and Dallas have an unusual number of outstanding museums. When the museums are considered together, as being part of a single great metropolitan region, the accumulated displays can hardly be surpassed anywhere. The Museum of Science and History is unique, both because of its concept and its exceptional design. Another unique Fort Worth museum is the Old West Museum, with its cowboy relics. One of the city's leading tourist attractions is the Carter Museum of Western Art, claiming the world's most important collection in its field. The new Kimball Art Museum should be included in any list, as well as the Fort Worth Art Center and C.M. Noble Planetarium, completing the site of the Civic Center. This also includes the Will Rogers Memorial Coliseum and Municipal Auditorium.

In the 187-acre (about 76-hectare) Fair Park are outstanding museums: Dallas Museum of Natural History; Dallas Museum of Fine Arts and the Art Institute of Dallas; the Texas Hall of State, with the Museum of Texas History; the Health and Science Museum and Planetarium; the Aquarium; and a botanical museum called the Garden Center. The Hall of State is considered one of the most magnificent historical buildings in America.

The annual State Fair at Fair Park is probably the largest in the nation. Also on the grounds of Fair Park is the renowned Cotton Bowl, scene of the annual bowl game.

Dallas' cultural advantages are further enhanced by the Dallas Theater Center, containing the only theater ever designed by Frank Lloyd Wright, a civic opera, and symphony orchestra.

Downtown Dallas

Symbol of Dallas' business leadership, Dallas Tower is one of the highest buildings west of the Mississippi. Neiman-Marcus department store has become a legend of the ultimate in shopping. One of the nation's new-style mammoth amusement parks is Six Flags Over Texas, a ten million dollar extravaganza of Texas history.

All of this is a far cry from the tiny trading post set up in 1840 by John Neely Bryan, whose first customers were Indians. This was the beginning of Dallas, which received its present name in 1842. Today on the Dallas County Courthouse lawn, visitors can see a good reproduction of the city's first building, the Bryan cabin.

Serving both Dallas and Fort Worth is Greater Southwest International Airport.

Fort Worth was named for William J. Worth, Mexican War hero. It began as a military outpost named Camp Worth. Founded in 1849, it grew rapidly and reached a population of 4,000, but hard times came, and the population declined to less than a thousand. One man said that the town was so dead he saw a panther sleeping in the main street. Loyal citizens of Fort Worth hooted at this. They laughingly called themselves Panthers and saw to it that their city made a solid and lasting comeback.

At Christmas season and during the Stock Show, Fort Worth is decorated in a most unusual display called "Paradise in the Sky." Every major building is outlined by amber lights, making a fairyland setting. The Fort Worth Zoo and Aquarium, Botanic Gardens, and the Albert Ruth Herbarium round out the enchantment of the city.

Weatherford is noted for its Chandor Gardens. These have been uniquely designed like a series of very dramatic outdoor rooms, rather than the usual garden pattern. Denton is the site of a three-story underground control center, the regional headquarters of the Office of Defense Mobilization. Eisenhower Birthplace State Park honors the famous American, born at nearby Denison, who became the first native of Texas to be President of the United States.

At Vernon the cowboys on cattle drives over the Western Trail had their last chance to put in supplies before crossing a huge, uninhabited area. Vernon is also headquarters for the well-known W.T. Waggoner Ranch of 500,000 acres (about 200,000 hectares). Another ranch, that of C.T. Watkins near Quanah, was famous for its Wolf Hunt, and Wolf City, a tent town, set up for this event. Quanah was "washed" into its position as county seat. If a man had his washing done in one place for six weeks, he was qualified to vote. In this way a large number of railroad workers qualified and voted for Quanah.

Those who would like to see a herd of longhorns as they looked in the old days will be interested in the herd being stocked at Fort Griffin State Park. There are few longhorns left anywhere else.

In addition to its academic achievement, Hardin-Simmons University at Abilene is noted for its fully outfitted Cowboy Band, which has played to enthusiastic audiences throughout Europe and the United States.

NORTHWEST AND THE PANHANDLE

Ragtown came into being as a headquarters for buffalo hunters. All the huts were made of hide, and there was even a sort of hotel of hides. As the community grew, its name was changed to Amarillo, a Spanish word meaning yellow. The promoter of the town liked the name so much he had all the houses painted yellow. Today, Amarillo is the metropolis of the Panhandle, noted especially for its livestock auctions, said to be the largest in the world.

Not far from Amarillo is Tascosa, once called queen of Texas ghost towns. It was a tough town, and twenty-eight graves are still visible on its boot hill. When the railroads passed Tascosa by, the town died. Only the belle of Tascosa, Frenchy McCormick, stayed on, to be near the grave of her husband, gambler Mickey McCormick; she did not leave until 1939. Tascosa has been revived in an unusual way. Today it is the home of Boys Ranch, founded by Amarillo businessmen to give a new start to boys who seem to have little chance to become good citizens without special help. About 300 boys from all over the country live there, and its respected alumni total more than 2,000.

One of the world's greatest ranches came into being when the state set aside more than 3,000,000 acres (about 1,200,000 hectares) of public land in the Panhandle to pay for building the state capitol. As the contractors went on with their work, they kept receiving more of the land for their pay, creating the XIT Ranch.

Tourists who happen to be in Shamrock on Labor Day may have a pleasant surprise; each one receives a free watermelon. One of the

Lake Meredith
McBride Canyon
in the fall.

largest and most interesting of Texas state parks is Palo Duro Canyon.

In order to have a patent for a new town, the sponsors of Matador had to swear that there were at least twenty establishments doing business in the town. Cowboys of the Matador Ranch began to open new businesses by setting a few cans of food or a bolt of cloth on a box, and so Matador became a merchandising center.

Lubbock, named in honor of Thomas S. Lubbock, is the largest metropolitan center of northwest Texas. In nearby MacKenzie State Park strong efforts are being made to save the prairie dogs from extinction. Almost a million visitors a year view the antics of these playful animals in their Prairie Dog Town.

THE WEST

Once the Pecos River was called the end of civilization. Judge Roy Bean administered the only law west of the Pecos. Today in the town of Pecos visitors can see a replica of the judge's store.

A creation of Pecos is known around the world. In 1884, foremen of various local ranches decided to celebrate the Fourth of July by putting on a contest for the local cowboys in riding, roping, and other cowboy skills. The contest was so successful it has been held ever since, and is generally thought to have been the first rodeo ever held.

Another western event originated in McCamey, where the world's first Rattlesnake Derby was held in 1936. A large crowd watched the "racers"—Drain Pipe, Wonder Boy, Slicker, Esmeralda, and others—compete for a $200 prize. Slicker was the winner, and the Derby became an annual event.

Odessa, tourist center for the Odessa Meteor Crater, also has a full-size reproduction of Shakespeare's Globe Theater.

Old Fort Davis, near Alpine, which stood guard against the fierce Apache raids, has since been made a National Historic Site. McDonald Observatory, with its 82-inch (about 208 centimeters) reflecting telescope, is also near Alpine. Operated jointly by the

80

University of Texas and University of Chicago, the telescope is one of the largest in the world. Nearby Indian Lodge Hotel is a unique structure, built like an ancient cliff-dweller adobe. Its handmade furniture is in Indian style.

THAT GRAND RIVER

El Paso and its twin on the Mexican side, Juarez, form the largest metropolitan area on the Mexican border. The El Paso area contains the oldest European town in Texas, Ysleta, with the oldest mission—Del Carmen—and the oldest parish church in the state—Socorro.

The region was first called *El Paso del Norte* by Juan de Oñate about 1598. Today El Paso has a tremendously growing population. In addition to its historic relics, it also has such ultra-modern sights as the guided missile and antiaircraft training center at Fort Bliss.

Near El Paso, on the top of Mt. Cristo Rey, stands the huge statue of Christ of the Rockies, with arms outstretched. Ten thousand people climbed the mountain to see it dedicated as an international peace monument. Another favorite mountain of the region is Mt. Franklin, with a breathtaking aerial tramway to its top, as well as a magnificent view of three states and two nations.

In this region some of the land titles date back to the earliest Spanish grants. Because land grants were measured with rawhide ropes, most landholders wanted their land measured on rainy days, because the rawhide stretched in wet weather.

South and east of El Paso, where the Rio Grande flows along in a vast horseshoe bend, lies one of America's last great wilderness areas—Big Bend National Park. Here, in places, the awesome walls of the canyon rise abruptly for 1,500 feet (about 457 meters) above the river. Its River Road is one of America's most scenic drives.

At the weather-beaten town of Langtry stands the restored saloon in which Judge Roy Bean administered the law with one law book and a six-shooter. His justice was often bizarre, but frequently fair. Sometimes a culprit's only fine would be a round of drinks for the

Boot Canyon and the "boot" in Big Bend National Park.

house, and the judge would quickly slip behind the bar to serve the thirsty crowd. The story is told that Bean renamed the town in honor of his favorite actress, Lily Langtry. On a cross-country rail trip, the famous actress made the conductor hold the train, carrying her special car, until she could visit the town bearing her name. Judge Bean had died before that time, however.

Laredo is the major international crossing along the entire United States-Mexican border and the chief point of entry into Mexico on the Pan-American Highway. Seven flags have flown over the city. The "extra" flag was that of the Republic of the Rio Grande. Just across the river, Nuevo Laredo is popular with visitors for its plazas, markets, gift shops, restaurants, nightclubs, and bull ring.

Historic Brownsville is the southernmost city in Texas. Its semi-tropical climate and its many Mexican influences are attractive to visitors. The annual Charro Days bring out Brownsville people in Mexican costumes in a happy fiesta.

CENTRAL-SOUTH

A memorial shaft at Goliad preserves the memory of those who were massacred there as they fought for Texas independence. Helena has given its name to a type of hand-to-hand combat called the Helena Duel, where two frontiersmen had their left wrists tied together and fought it out with short-bladed knives.

One of Texas' most interesting communities is New Braunfels, still almost as German as it is American. Here, on a hill, the founder, Prince Carl von Solms-Braunfels, built his castle headquarters, manned by velvet-clad courtiers—royal style on the Texas prairie— until he gave up and returned to Germany. When 5,000 Germans came to join the settlement, they found no transportation. Many attempted the long walk from the coast. As many as 2,000 of the German pioneers are thought to have died of heat, disease, hunger, and exposure. The road to New Braunfels is lined with German graves.

San Marcos is noted for its large spring, in which a submarine theater offers an underwater show to spectators.

Austin, capital of Texas, has many distinctions. Its great domed capitol is second in size only to the Capitol at Washington, D.C. The

The Capitol Building in Austin.

building was completed in 1888, and is especially noted for its heroic paintings by W.H. Huddle. Built at a "cost" of 3,000,000 acres (about 1,200,000 hectares) of land, it is the only capitol ever financed in such a manner. An architectural contrast is Texas' impressive modern Supreme Court Building. The governor's mansion is a stately southern colonial home built in 1855.

Most visitors are moved emotionally by many of the displays in the State Library and Archives Building at Austin, but particularly by the original document of the Texas Declaration of Independence.

The capital, named for Stephen F. Austin, is a planned city of wide and handsome sweep. One of its particular prides was its system of lighting. Complete illumination, like artificial moonlight, provided by twenty-seven "light towers" dotting the city. One of the wonders of its day when installed in 1895, it was then the only system of its kind in the world.

Other points of interest in Austin are: the grave of Stephen F. Austin; the O. Henry Museum, in memory of the famous short story writer who lived and wrote there; the Elizabet Ney Museum; the gigantic Memorial Stadium; and the University of Texas. The popular Lyndon B. Johnson Library is the first established at a university.

Temple is a leading hospital center, and Marlin is noted for its health facilities and fine mineral wells.

The Hueco Indians gave Waco its distinctive name. It is particularly noted for Baylor University's Carroll Library Browning Room, said to have the world's largest collection of original works of Robert and Elizabeth Barrett Browning. All of the Browning first editions are there except *Pauline*. Beautiful stained glass windows illustrate several of the poems. The region has come a long way since the time Dr. A.M. Barnett arrived in 1851 with his family, traded two quilts and a rag carpet for 10 acres (about 4 hectares) of land and began his practice there.

Near Burnet are the famous Longhorn Caverns, once a favorite hide-out for Indians and outlaws. During one uprising Robert E. Lee drove a group of Indians into the cave to capture them. He did not know there were six exits, and the Indians escaped. These caverns housed a powder magazine during the Civil War.

The skyline of Austin.

Picturesque Fredericksburg is another thoroughly German community. The Gillespie County Fair, held each August, is the oldest county fair in Texas. Many traditional German festivals are held. The most famous, more than 100 years old, is the Easter Fires Pageant. The young people of the community prepare blazing bonfires, which dot the countryside during the night. The Pioneer Museum and Country Store are other attractions.

Johnson City and Uvalde are interesting as homes of two former vice-presidents of the United States, one of whom also became president. Lyndon B. Johnson's Texas White House ranch can be seen from the Ranch Road just off Highway 290. At Albert is the school where the youthful Johnson said, "Someday I'm going to be President of the United States." The Uvalde home of Vice-President John Nance Garner is now a memorial museum. Garner State Park is to the north.

Castorville, near San Antonio, is another Texan town giving the interesting impression of a foreign community. This French settlement, with its quaint architecture of Alsace, is a landmark of the state.

CITY OF SAINT ANTHONY OF PADUA

San Antonio is one of the most distinctive cities in America. In May, 1718, Father Antonio de San Buenaventura Olivares founded Mission San Antonio de Valero, named in honor of Saint Anthony of Padua. He could not have foreseen that this would become one of the best-known missions in America, and the most popular tourist attraction in Texas.

Just how the chapel of this mission became known as the Alamo is not certain, but probably it came about because of its use at one time as barracks by Spanish soldiers from Alamo del Parras. In 1793 the mission buildings were abandoned, and the Alamo became a roofless ruin. Because its thick walls seemed to offer the greatest protection, it was chosen for the immortal stand by its brave defenders. The Alamo has been restored to much of its original condition, and now remains a scarred and weathered monument to Texas' heroic past. It is cared for lovingly by the Daughters of the Republic of Texas. The Alamo museum has a large display of interesting mementoes.

In the plaza outside the Alamo stands the Alamo Cenotaph, honoring the heroes of the battle who fell in the old chapel nearby. Portrait statues of James Bowie, James Bonham, William Travis, and Davy Crockett are featured, and the names of all the defenders are carved in the granite slabs. The Alamo defenders are buried in San Fernando Cathedral in San Antonio.

Many other missions were founded in the area, which became one of the great mission centers. Today these early missions provide a

Downtown San Antonio.

*The River Walk
in San Antonio.*

fascinating reminder of the past. Best preserved is Mission Concepcion. Mission San Jose was known as the most beautiful, most prosperous, and best fortified of all Texas missions, with the nickname Queen of the Missions.

The historic city of San Antonio lived under the flags of France, Spain, Mexico, Republic of Texas, Confederate States, and United States. It is laid out roughly like a giant spider web.

San Antonio's careful restoration of its historic past makes it one of the most picturesque cities anywhere. Hemisphere Plaza, site of the 1968 World's Fair, offers many delights, including the outstanding Institute of Texan Cultures, where history is a fascinating adventure; the striking 750-foot (about 229-meter) Tower of the

Americas; and La Villita, a reconstruction of a 200-year-old Spanish town.

The River Walk is one of the most delightful experiences of the Americas. Here the sightseeing barges become outdoor cafés at night. Shops of great charm, dining terraces, hotels, and beautiful landscaping are concentrated here for the visitors' delight.

Also on the San Antonio River is Arneson River Theater, one of the most unusual anywhere. Its stage is on one bank of the river, and the audience sits on the opposite bank.

The Spanish governor's palace is the only early, fine Spanish home remaining in Texas.

Brackenridge Park, one of the country's outstanding city parks, is the home of San Antonio's enormous zoo, Witte Memorial Museum, Chinese Garden, and Sunken Garden and Theater. McNay Art Institute is a cultural center of the city.

San Antonio has long been known as one of the great military centers of the country. There are four air force bases—Lackland, Kelly, Brooks, and Randolph. The Aerospace Medical Center was the first institution in the world to be established for the sole purpose of studying space medicine. Today, other complex problems of the space age are considered there, too. Fort Sam Houston is headquarters for the Fourth United States Army, covering a five-state area.

The old Quadrangle of Fort Sam Houston, built between 1876 and 1879, is one of the city's most interesting spots. Above its stern and massive walls looms an 88-foot (about 27-meter) medieval clock tower. During the imprisonment there of the Apache Chief, Geronimo, with his braves in 1886, some of the Indians decided to climb to the top of the tower. When the clock chimed, they scrambled down in panic at this mighty magic of the white man.

Most elaborate of all Texas fiestas is San Antonio's Fiesta of San Antonio, held each spring. This is a week-long spectacle, punctuated by parades, including an illuminated nighttime procession of decorated boats winding down the San Antonio River.

Those who see this festival are reminded again of the incredibly rich heritage America has received from other countries, of which Spain and Mexico are among the most prominent.

Handy Reference Section

Instant Facts

Became the 28th state, December 29, 1845
Capital—Austin, founded 1839
Nickname—The Lone Star State
Motto—Friendship (from Indian *Tejas,* "friends")
State bird—Mockingbird
State flower—Bluebonnet *(Lupinus texensis)*
State tree—Pecan
State animal—none officially—Longhorn, popularly
State gem—Topaz
State song—"Texas, Our Texas"
Area—262,130 square miles (678,914 square kilometers)
Greatest length (north to south)—800 miles (1,287 kilometers)
Greatest width (east to west)—775 miles (1,247 kilometers)
Highest point—8,751 feet (2,667 meters), Guadalupe Peak
Lowest point—Sea level
Number of counties—254
Coastline—367 miles (591 kilometers)
Population—12,847,000 (1980 projection)
Population density—42 persons per square mile (16 persons per square kilometer)
                  1970 census
Rank in density—33rd
Birthrate—18.9 per 1,000
Physicians per 100,000—123
Principal cities—

Houston	1,232,802 (1970 census)
Dallas	844,401
San Antonio	654,153
Fort Worth	393,476
El Paso	322,261
Austin	251,808
Corpus Christi	204,525
Lubbock	149,101
Amarillo	127,010
Beaumont	117,548

You Have a Date with History

1519—First European, de Piñeda, explores, maps
1528—De Vaca shipwrecked, began explorations
1541—Coronado searches for wealth
1598—Oñate enters Texas
1682—First permanent settlement, Ysleta, founded
1685—LaSalle establishes French Fort St. Louis
1690—Beginning of Spanish missions—San Francisco de Los Tejas
1718—Mission San Antonio de Valero (the Alamo) founded
1817—Pirate Jean Lafitte controls coast
1821—First American settlers brought by Stephen Austin
1830—Mexican law limits further United States settlers
1833—Convention at San Felipe
1836—Texas becomes independent Republic
1839—Austin founded as Capital
1845—Statehood
1851—First railroad begun
1861—Secession passed, Houston deposed
1865—Last battle fought, Palmito Hill
1870—Texas readmitted to Union
1876—Current state constitution adopted
1883—University of Texas admits students
1888—State Capitol completed
1900—Galveston destroyed
1901—Spindletop, first major oil discovery
1910—First official army air flight, San Antonio
1917—Governor Ferguson impeached, removed
1936—Centennial Exposition, Dallas
1937—New London school disaster
1947—Texas City explosion
1953—Tidelands title to Texas
1963—President John F. Kennedy assassinated, Dallas; Lyndon Johnson becomes president
1964—Manned Spacecraft Center completed
1970—Employment in Texas approaches four million
1972—Barbara Jordan becomes first Southern black woman elected to the U.S. House
1973—Manned Spacecraft Center renamed Lyndon B. Johnson Space Center
1975—Joan Winn becomes first black woman judge in Texas

Thinkers, Doers, Fighters

People of renown who have been associated with Texas

Austin, Moses
Austin, Stephen
Bean, Roy
Borden, Gail
Bowie, James
Chandor, Douglas
Cliburn, Van
Crockett, David
Eisenhower, Dwight David
Garner, John Nance
Gates, John Warne
Hays, Jack
Hornsby, Rogers
House, W.M.
Houston, Sam

Johnson, Jack
Johnson, Lyndon Baines
King, Richard
Lavender, Eugenie
Lucas, A.F.
Martin, Albert
Murphy, Audie
Ney, Elizabet
Nimitz, Chester W.
Parker, Quanah
Perry, George Sessions
Rayburn, Sam
Stillwell, Arthur Edwards
Travis, William Barret

Governors

J. Pinckney Henderson 1846-1847
Albert C. Horton 1847
George T. Wood 1847-1849
P. Hansbrough Bell 1849-1853
J.W. Henderson 1853-1853
Elisha M. Pease 1853-1857
Hardin R. Runnels 1857-1859
Sam Houston 1859-1861
Edward Clark 1861-1861
Francis R. Lubbock 1861-1863
Pendleton Murrah 1863-1865
Andrew J. Hamilton 1865-1866
James W. Throckmorton 1866-1867
Elisha M. Pease 1867-1869
Edmund J. Davis 1870-1874
Richard Coke 1874-1876
Richard B. Hubbard 1876-1879
Oran M. Roberts 1879-1883
John Ireland 1883-1887
Lawrence Sullivan Ross 1887-1891
James Stephen Hogg 1891-1895

Charles A. Culberson 1895-1899
Joseph D. Sayers 1899-1903
S.W.T. Lanham 1903-1907
Thos. Mitchell Campbell 1907-1911
Oscar Branch Colquitt 1911-1915
James E. Ferguson 1915-1917
William Pettus Hobby 1917-1921
Pat Morris Neff 1921-1925
Miriam A. Ferguson 1925-1927
Dan Moody 1927-1931
Ross S. Sterling 1931-1933
Miriam A. Ferguson 1933-1935
James V. Allred 1935-1939
W. Lee O'Daniel 1939-1941
Coke R. Stevenson 1941-1947
Beauford H. Jester 1947-1949
Allan Shivers 1949-1957
Price Daniel 1957-1963
John Connally 1963-1969
Preston Smith 1969-1973
Dolph Brisco 1973-1979
William Perry Clements 1979-

Index

92

93

94

95

PICTURE CREDITS

ABOUT THE AUTHOR

With the publication of his first book for school use when he was twenty, **Allan Carpenter** began a career as an author that has spanned more than 135 books. After teaching in the public schools of Des Moines, Mr. Carpenter began his career as an educational publisher at the age of twenty-one when he founded the magazine *Teachers Digest*. In the field of educational periodicals, he was responsible for many innovations. During his many years in publishing, he has perfected a highly organized approach to handling large volumes of factual material: after extensive traveling and having collected all possible materials, he systematically reviews and organizes everything. From his apartment high in Chicago's John Hancock Building, Allan recalls, "My collection and assimilation of materials on the states and countries began before the publication of my first book." Allan is the founder of Carpenter Publishing House and of Infordata International, Inc., publishers of *Issues in Education* and *Index to U. S. Government Periodicals.* When he is not writing or traveling, his principal avocation is music. He has been the principal bassist of many symphonies, and he managed the country's leading non-professional symphony for twenty-five years.